The Spider Web Philosophy

The Spider Web Philosophy

CATCH YOUR DREAMS

Dwight H Pullen

Aki Jamal Durham

Wesley G Pullen

Greg El

First Edition

DAWG Media, LLC
523 Halsey Ave
Forest Hills, PA 152221

ISBN 13: 9780986187308

ISBN: 0986187305

Special thanks to our families for their unwavering support of this endeavor and of our need to come together as a group for rest and replenishment. Your willingness to give us this necessary time and space enabled us to find something so worthwhile that it gave us not only a better quality of life but also an undeniable desire to share it with the world.

We would also like to thank Valentine K. Brkich for taking our four unique voices and successfully merging them into one.

"The means to gain happiness is to throw out from oneself like a spider in all directions an adhesive web of love, and to catch in it all that comes."

—*Count Leo Nikolayevich Tolstoy*

Contents

Foreword

When I first met Greg El in Philadelphia in March 2012, I was honored that he and his fellow coauthors wanted me to write the foreword for their new book, *The Spider Web Philosophy*. After I had the opportunity to read the prepress draft of the book, I was so proud of how these four successful young men had taken my thoughts on the power of connectedness and built upon them to develop their truly life-changing philosophy.

Through my company, FraserNet Inc., we teach people that knowledge is valuable and that wisdom is priceless. We also show them that in this new age of interdependence it's essential to be both supportive and supportable. If you want to make an impact on people in your life, if you want to find success in your endeavors, you have to be willing to serve up your wisdom. And this is exactly what Greg, Dwight, Aki, and Wes are doing through the tools they share in this important book.

There is power in connectedness; make no mistake about it. When we try to achieve success on our own, we waste valuable time, energy, and resources. *The Spider Web Philosophy* provides a whole new way of getting what you want out of life. It shows you how to catch your dreams instead of chasing them down. It provides substance to what I've been telling people for years: as a divided people, we are powerless; the power comes through connectedness.

Today, with social media and networking being such a huge part of our lives, we can see how sharing ideas and wisdom with others can have an enormous and immediate impact. However, these tools, when used irresponsibly and without careful thought, can also have negative reper-cussions. *The Spider Web Philosophy* addresses this by teaching you how to connect with others in a thoughtful, responsible, accountable way that yields positive results for all parties and creates a healthy environment that promotes success, balance, and overall happiness.

I'm so proud to be a part of this important movement, and I know that it will help you catch everything you want out of life.

George C. Fraser
Founder, FraserNet.com

Introduction

Have you ever really looked at a spider web?

We've all seen them, strung up between bushes in the yard, or maybe in the corner of the basement, dangling from the rafters. Maybe you've gotten an unintentional close-up look as you walked through one on a wooded trail, the silk wrapping around your head while you scrambled to free yourself from the sticky entanglement.

But have you ever taken time to truly see a spider web? The intricate, systematic construction, the purposeful design, with threads radiating out from the center and crisscrossing the spiral, again and again, like tiny support beams holding the web securely in place. It is beauty and purpose perfectly intertwined. It's a wonder of nature.

The spider web is not only beautiful; it's practical. It's the ideal trap, a model of efficiency, fashioned over millions of years of evolutionary improvement. What's more amazing is that it only takes the spider a few hours to create this one-of-a-kind masterpiece.

For years scientists have been studying spiders and their webs, trying unsuccessfully to duplicate the incredibly strong silk that spiders use to make the frame lines that anchor their webs and suspend them in midair. This natural protein is one of the strongest and most flexible materials known. In fact, some silk is as strong as Kevlar—the material used to make bulletproof vests.

Now you're probably thinking, this is all very interesting, but what in the world does a spider web have to do with me? More than you'd think. Just ask George C. Fraser.

In 2005, Fraser, the chairman, CEO, and founder of FraserNet Inc., spoke at the State of the Black Union conference in Lithonia, Georgia, which focused on the economic disparity that exists in the African American community. During the conference, Mr. Fraser took out a chart showing a series of dots that symbolized this disparity.

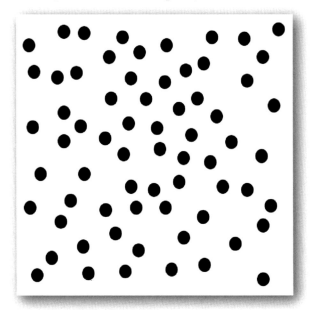

By themselves, said Fraser, African Americans have done some wonderful things; however, as a group the African American community remains disconnected and powerless. Then he flipped the chart to show those same individual dots connected by lines. "This is where all the power is," said Fraser.

The image was that of the perfect network: a spider web.

The spider web is the ideal representation of the strength and power found through interconnectedness. And when you harness its strength and power and apply it to your life, amazing things can happen. You can *catch* your dreams.

There's an old Ethiopian proverb that says, "When spider webs unite, they can tie down a lion." Think about that for a moment. Sometimes in life, that's what your goals and dreams can seem like—a fearsome, untamable lion. And there you are, a lonesome spider, a minuscule speck of dust in comparison to the formidable king of the jungle. No matter how hard you try to catch the lion by yourself, you keep failing. It's not for lack of effort; it's just that you are outsized and outmatched.

But when you connect with others through authentic relationships— that is, ones that are transparent, honest, and nonjudgmental—when you are given access to their skills, wisdom, and resources, you can grow and strengthen your web until it becomes a giant, far-reaching, impenetrable web that will help you *catch* whatever you want out of life.

When spider webs unite, they can tie down a lion!

A web, simply put, is a network. It is a series of points connected by silk that forms a powerful, effective tool for accomplishing a goal—for catching something. Why do you think the Internet is called the World Wide *Web*? It's an electronic web for connecting people and sharing information.

If you consider your own network as a web, your connections are the individual dots or points where the lines of silk come together. These points may represent your family members, friends, coworkers, church members, business partners, neighbors, and so on, and they all represent other "spiders" in the larger web of your life.

Maybe you've never thought of spider webs in this way before. That's OK. One of our goals in this book is to open your eyes and your mind to a new way of looking at things, a way that will help you get where you want to be in life by showing you how to *catch* your aspirations instead of trying to chase them down. We want to help you build the perfect web, one that will take you to the next level and help you find and achieve your true purpose in life.

When George Fraser used his spider-web analogy, he was speaking to the African American community. But there is a deeper message there, one for all races and all genders. As individuals, we *may* find happiness and success, and we *may* get what we want out of this life. But when we are united, when we collaborate and cooperate with others and tap into their skills and resources, our chances of finding success and catching our dreams grow exponentially.

You have many webs in your life. Your family is a web. Your coworkers and professional connections—another web. Your friendships form another kind of web, and so do the members of your church family. Each of these webs is unique and important in its own way, and each serves a different purpose.

But can any of these webs alone get you to where you want to be in your life? Your family web may provide unconditional support, but would you trust your family members to make your career decisions for you? And what about your friends? Some you can count on for anything, others, not so much. Your church family may share your same faith and values, but do they really know you and what makes you tick? And as for your professional connections, would you trust them to give you marital advice? Probably not.

But what if you had one rock-solid web that was anchored by your most authentic relationships, those individuals who know you inside and out—your strengths and weaknesses, your passions and goals? What if you had one focused web—a series of mutually beneficial relationships—with a solid, dependable core where you could simultaneously rest, replenish, and receive? With this kind of web, you could stop wasting valuable energy chasing the wrong "prey" and instead begin to *catch* your dreams, goals, and aspirations.

This is very real. It has worked for each of us, and it can work for you, too. We call it the Spider Web Philosophy™, and it has three critical attributes:

> **The Web**—Identifying the Network: Your Authentic Relationships at Work
>
> **Self-Awareness**—Personal Mastery: Understanding Purpose and Passion
>
> **The Master Mind**—Accountability and Support: Your Personal Board of Directors

The Spider Web Philosophy is a paradigm shift. It's like that little blue pill in the movie *The Matrix* that opens one's mind to a new way of thinking. It is founded on the principles developed by individuals like Napoleon Hill and others who recognized the incredible power of connectedness. By tapping their knowledge and synthesizing it into a unified, practical, purposeful philosophy, we have created a system that has proven to be invaluable in our lives, bringing each of us success, happiness, and fulfillment.

And we know it can do the same for you.

This book is meant to serve as a step-by-step guide to the Spider Web Philosophy. In the coming chapters, we will:

- Illustrate the power, efficiency, and effectiveness of the spider and its web and how we can benefit from mimicking the strategy the spider employs.
- Help you strategically create and place your web so that you can catch your dreams and aspirations.

- Share powerful stories about how this philosophy has helped each of us achieve greater-than-average success in various aspects of our lives.
- Warn you about the obstacles and challenges you'll face along the way and give you the tools to meet these challenges head-on and with conviction.
- Show you how to manage, maintain, and sustain your web in order to get the most out of it.
- Spotlight individuals who have found success and fulfillment in their lives through living the principles of the Spider Web Philosophy.

Along the way, we'll also have a little fun as we look at spiders and their webs and appreciate them for the amazing evolutionary wonders that they are. At the end of each chapter, we'll provide a summary of that chapter's main takeaways, just to make sure you didn't miss the important things. We'll also provide some questions and action items that will help you build your web as you make your way through the book.

We don't claim to be experts on spiders. Far from it. We are, however, relationship experts. We have seen firsthand how fostering authentic relationships and then leveraging those relationships can help you determine your passions and purpose and help you get what you want out of life. We've all lived and continue to live the Spider Web Philosophy and have reaped the benefits of dedicating ourselves to it. We believe in the power of this philosophy, and we have the tangible proof of its effectiveness. Now we wish to share this power with you and show you that, when you believe in it and adhere to its principles, when you live your life with purpose and open your mind and heart to God's will, amazing things can happen.

Amazing things will happen.

Chapter 1

HIGH GRADE SILK –
*The Primary Ingredient
for an Effective
Web:*

QUALITY

RELATIONSHIPS

It's Not Who You Know

You've heard it before: It's not what you know; it's *who* you know. In other words, it doesn't matter how smart you are or where you went to college or how much experience you have. If you want to succeed in this world, if you want to get off the sidelines and into the game, you simply have to have the right connections. It's not what you know; it's *who* you know.

Or is it?

What if we told you this old adage was incomplete? That it's not really about whom you know or even who knows you?

Say, for example, you have this friend, James, who knows the CEO of a company you've desperately been trying to land a job with. So you give your friend James your résumé and ask him get it in front of his boss. Now what? Well, maybe the CEO sees your résumé and sees something that she likes. Maybe she thinks you'd be a great addition to the company. Maybe she respects James's opinion and decides to bring you in for an interview. The key to this situation is, what is James saying you are capable of accomplishing? James will now be responsible to the CEO for selling your skill set and abilities. The CEO is going to ask James to differentiate you from anyone else that could apply for this opportunity (if an opportunity even exists). So now we have to ask the question—what does James think about you? Are you aware of what James is saying about you without your knowledge? If James sells you to the CEO as a great individual contributor, and you desired to manage an entire team…it will be quite difficult for you now to sell yourself higher than what a referral has recommended.

Maybe the CEO never even sees your résumé because James does not know how to sell you. Or maybe the CEO sees it, but since she doesn't know you from Adam, she couldn't care less about you or your current situation. For all you know, she might not think very highly of your friend at all. In the end your résumé ends up in the circular file, and you're out of luck. The key again is that the CEO is going to leverage what James says about you as the key reference as to who you are and what value you can offer to the organization.

Either one of these scenarios is possible, really. But once you give your résumé to your friend, it's out of your control. Do you really want to leave your life and your dreams up to fate? What confirmation or specific understanding do you currently have that allows you to fully comprehend how a particular friend views the skill set you have and its impact to a particular area?

The truth is…it's not just about what you know. And you certainly can't pin your hopes on *who* you know. *It's about who knows you and what they think about you and the talent you bring to the table to assist them in accomplishing their goals and objectives.* Simply put…you have to have a skill set, knowledge base, or quality of character that people see as valuable, and they must view you as a critical asset to accomplishing a particular goal or series of goals. So the old adage of who you know is simply not enough any longer. We have to be strategic in making an impression to others about the talent, understanding, and sensitivity we bring to the table and how those particular qualities can mean the difference for a particular person, company, or situation.

Authenticity

The spider invests everything into its web. In a spider's web, if the connections aren't strong, the web will be weak and ineffective. The same goes for you. If your connections—your relationships—aren't authentic, they're of no use to you. You have to make a real investment, just as the spider does. Authenticity is the key here. In order for a relationship to have any value to you, it has to be reciprocal. It has to be real, transparent, honest, and nonjudgmental. It has to be authentic. There has to be a certain chemistry between you and the other person, some special connection where each person thinks and acts with the other's best interest in mind. These are the ingredients of authenticity. When the authenticity is missing, the relationship is of little or no value to you. But when your web is made up of these types of relationships, magic can happen. The authenticity must extend to how transparent the connection can be in assessing and detailing what strengths you have and what weaknesses you have as well.

Take Aki, for example. Aki used to give group presentations for real-estate and mortgage professionals. In these presentations he would tell them how to stay in constant contact with their sphere of influence so that they could always have a pool of repeat clients and referrals. During his twenty-minute pitch, Aki would share what he likes to call his "Jerome Bettis Story."

You may be familiar with Jerome "The Bus" Bettis as a former running back for the Pittsburgh Steelers and recent NFL Hall of Fame inductee, who at the time of his retirement was the fourth leading rusher in NFL history. He's also a fairly successful media personality. Aki actually knows Jerome. Jerome's younger brother, John, is a businessman in Pittsburgh, and he and Aki have done business together on several occasions. John has introduced Aki to Jerome in both personal and professional settings. Jerome also has a former college-football teammate named Cliff who is a mutual friend of Aki's. Cliff has also introduced Aki to Jerome several times.

Aki happens to have some media aspirations of his own. He's hosted a radio show in the past and would like to get back on the air someday. He also does some acting and voice-over work and even some event hosting. Someone like Jerome Bettis could easily open some doors for Aki in that arena, given his current occupation as a sports commentator on national television. So it would make sense for Aki to ask Jerome for help, right?

Not necessarily.

The problem is, Jerome doesn't really *know* Aki. In spite of the dozen or more times they've shaken hands and shared pleasantries, Jerome has yet to commit Aki to memory. Being a sports celebrity, Jerome is always being approached by fans trying to get an autograph or take a picture with him. To him, Aki is just another face in the crowd. In fact, the last few times he and Jerome have met, Aki has let him know that he didn't need to feel bad about not remembering him. Aki understands that Jerome cannot possibly differentiate him from the hundreds of other people he meets every week.

You see, Jerome has yet to form an opinion of Aki, good or bad. There is no *authenticity* in their relationship. Therefore, how could Aki ever expect Jerome to want to do anything for him?

Remember: *It's not what you know. It's not even who you know. It's who knows you and what they think about you!*

Whenever Aki used to share this story, he consistently got even the most apathetic and disinterested people in the room to perk up and start paying attention. It connected with them. They understood that, in order to succeed, you need to focus on gradually forming meaningful, authentic relationships and then regularly maintain those relationships, so that what others think about you is what you want them to think about you.

When you're cultivating authentic relationships, you have to recognize and understand the other person's unique passions and goals. If you want someone to help you catch your aspirations, that person has to know you on a personal level. The clearer you are about what you want—your goals and passions—the easier it will be for someone to help you realize your ambitions.

In *How to Win Friends and Influence People* (1936), Dale Carnegie said this about when he used to go fishing in Maine during the summer:

> Personally I am very fond of strawberries and cream, but I have found that for some strange reason, fish prefer worms. So when I went fishing, I didn't think about what I wanted. I thought about what they wanted. I didn't bait the hook with strawberries and cream. Rather, I dangled a worm or grasshopper in front of the fish and said: "Wouldn't you like to have that?" Why not use the same common sense when fishing for people?

In other words, if you want to develop authentic relationships with people, first find out what *they* are looking for, and then figure out how you can help them find it.

A few years back, Wes was working for a software company that sold a deal to the federal government. One of the company's key decision makers, a man named Jim, asked Wes to come on-site regularly to perform demonstrations and general maintenance on the software. In time, Jim and Wes built a strong professional relationship with each other.

Over the next few years, Wes did his best to help Jim him in any way he could. He performed demos for other high-ranking officials in the government, he took part in conference calls to assist Jim and his team with the software, he provided on-site professional services when things went wrong, and he handled a host of other emergencies that came up from time to time. Did we mention that Wes wasn't getting paid a single dime for any of this? But that was OK. In his book, *Leadership GOLD*, John C. Maxwell says, "If you are willing to sacrifice financially on the front end for the possibility of greater potential, you are almost always given greater chances for higher rewards—including financially." Wes wasn't thinking of himself at the time. His only objective was to do his best to help Jim and his team so that they could be successful. Wes wanted to make sure that when Jim called for help, he'd be there for him.

Jim's gratitude for Wes's service was immeasurable, and it helped them build an authentic, lasting business relationship and friendship. This relationship led to other opportunities, and soon Jim was calling on Wes again, this time to begin a company and fulfill a long-term federal contract that allowed Wes to work part-time and match the income he generated working full-time.

What do other people think about you? Can you really even know for sure? Maybe not. But what you can do is make sure that you're doing everything in your power to ensure that, when someone has an opinion of you, it's (at the very least) an accurate one and (as much as possible) a positive one.

Cultivating strong, authentic relationships over time and then leveraging those relationships to catch your dreams—that's what the Spider Web Philosophy is all about.

Your Web versus the World Wide Web

There is no doubt that the Internet is a powerful networking tool. Hundreds of millions of people connect through it each day through social-networking applications like LinkedIn, Twitter, and Facebook. But when it comes to you and your goals, is the Internet really the most effective way for you to build authentic relationships?

LinkedIn has become the preferred professional-networking tool on the Internet. In fact, many people now forego a résumé altogether and instead opt for an online record of their work experience via their personal LinkedIn profiles. It provides a simple yet effective way to connect with other professionals in your particular line of work, giving you a way to meet people through your connections' connections.

Twitter has changed the way we connect with each other and share information, and it enables us to share that information faster than ever before. Limiting you to just 140 characters, Twitter forces you to be brief and concise while sharing useful information instantly with people around the globe. It also helps people build personal and professional platforms—e-personalities, if you will—that help in attracting others and making connections.

And then there's Facebook, the King Kong of social networking. With almost a billion users and counting, it has become the place for people to connect and share everything about their jobs, their personal life, news, things they find on the web, and more.

In addition to these, there are Google+ and MySpace and Ning and YouTube and Meetup and…well, you get the picture.

So with all these powerful social-networking tools that enable us to instantly connect with people online, with just the click of a mouse, why should you worry about building authentic relationships? Want your voice to be heard? Just post your thoughts on your Facebook status, and people will be begging for more. Want to get your book published? Just tweet the editor at that big-name New York publishing house, and before you know it, you'll be signing a three-book contract. Want to land the job of your dreams? Connect with as many people as you can out on LinkedIn, and the job offers will come flying in. Right?

Not exactly.

You may have one thousand "friends" on Facebook, but what's it really *doing* for you? LinkedIn may be helping you connect with others in your field, but how *reliable* are these connections? And although it can be thrilling to make a one-to-one connection with an industry insider via Twitter, how *authentic* is that connection? Why would that person want to go out of his or her way to help you?

So does this mean that social-networking tools have no value to you? Of course not. When used appropriately and toward a specific purpose, these tools can provide some real value to getting you where you want to be. The trick is to not let them become time-consuming procrastination traps where you're just swapping gossip or the latest viral video. When you spend your time using these tools, concentrate on building purpose-driven relationships and connections.

Take Facebook. If you do nothing but try to increase your number of "likes," you're not really working toward building authentic relationships. But if you use it to connect with people to whom you have something to offer and then focus on *their needs* first, Facebook can play a part in fostering authentic connections that will eventually pay dividends.

The same goes for Twitter, LinkedIn, and any other social-media platform. Use these powerful tools to find the types of connections you need to get you where you want to go, and then find out what you can offer that's of value to those connections.

In other words, take advantage of the incredible networking power of the Internet and social media, and use them to develop credibility for your own personal web. These online vehicles can take you far, if you remember that the people you are riding with are more important that what you are riding in. Just be careful: the World Wide Web can be a pretty sticky place.

Chapter 1 Takeaways
So let's review:

- It's not about what you know or who you know. It's about who knows you and what they think about you and the talent you bring to the table to assist them in accomplishing their goals.
- Make sure that you're doing everything in your power to ensure that, when someone has an opinion of you, it is always genuine and positive.
- You must cultivate strong, authentic relationships over time and then leverage those relationships to catch your dreams, goals, and ambitions.
- In order for someone to help you catch your aspirations, that person first has to recognize and respect your passions.
- In order for a relationship to have any value to you, it has to be reciprocal. It has to be real, transparent, honest, and nonjudgmental. It has to be authentic.
- The World Wide Web and social media can help you foster authentic relationships, but only when used properly and carefully.

Worksheet #1

What do you think others think of you when they first meet you?

What would you like others to think about you?

List the people with whom you have truly authentic relationships.

How did you cultivate these relationships?

List five people with whom you'd like to cultivate authentic relationships.

How much time do you spend on social media every day, and what value
has it yielded toward reaching your goals?

Think of three small steps you can take this week to start to cultivate new,
authentic relationships.

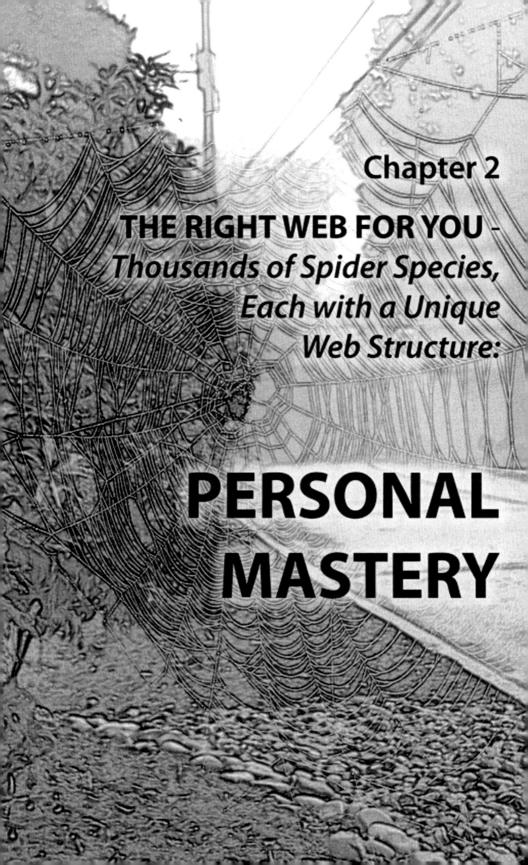

Chapter 2

THE RIGHT WEB FOR YOU –
*Thousands of Spider Species,
Each with a Unique
Web Structure:*

PERSONAL

MASTERY

J ust as there are many different species of spider—over forty thousand—there are also many different types of webs.

Take the orb-spider's web, for example, which resembles a wheel with spokes radiating outward. These webs are orderly, and each line of silk has a specific and important purpose. Then there are sheet webs, which resemble little sheets or canopies. You may have seen these types of webs scattered all over your yard on a dewy morning. There are many other types as well, such as gum-footed webs, horizontal-line webs, triangle webs—the list goes on and on.

So what type of "web" do you need? Well, that depends on what you want to catch. Your connections and relationships in your web should be reliable, authentic, and catered to your specific goals and aspirations. Most of all, your web must be unique to you. It has to be carefully planned and designed to fit you and your particular ambitions. Each of those forty thousand spider species has a unique system for catching what it needs to sustain itself, and you must create the same for yourself.

In short, if you want to catch the right opportunities for you and reach your full potential, you have to focus on creating and growing a purpose-built web that is custom designed for you.

What Type of Spider Are You?

In your lifetime you've probably come across many different types of spiders. In the United States alone, there are over three thousand species, and each has a particular way of doing things.

Trap-door spiders, for example, dig burrows in the ground and seal the opening with a hinged lid or trap door. Then they sit and wait until dinner comes by. Jumping spiders hop around when hunting and can leap up to forty times their own body length, anchoring themselves with a bungee-cord-type line of silk. Nursery web spiders spin webs specifically to care for and protect their young. Then of course you have orb-web spiders, which spin those magnificent, wheel-shaped creations.

Different spider spiders even target different sets of prey. While many of them rely on insects as their primary source of food, some actually trap small mammals and even use other spiders for sustenance.

We can all think of some people who feed off of their own kind as well.

Humans, like spiders, come in all different shapes, sizes, and colors. We come from different backgrounds and different parts of the world. Each of us is comfortable in our own particular surroundings, has his or her particular way of doing things, and is sustained and fulfilled by different things. Some of us are solitary, while some of us are more social and prefer to have many relationships. That's the beauty of humanity. God made us all different. He gave us each our own unique personality, skill set, talents, desires, and passions. And when you're able to recognize and embrace these personal preferences, you open the door to a happier, more fulfilling, more successful life.

Each person has a purpose in this life. You are here for a reason. Before you can achieve any level of success in your life, you must first know yourself. You must recognize and embrace your purpose. What are your passions? What is important to you? Without introspection and self-assessment, you cannot fully understand yourself; you cannot know exactly what you want out of life.

If you want to be successful, if you want to find happiness, you have to be confident in knowing who you are and what you represent to those around you. What is your role in your family? In your friendships? If you belong to any groups, clubs, or organizations, how do the other members see you, and what role do you play for them?

It's important to know not only who you are but also *why* **y**ou are. As we said before, God created you for a reason. He purposed and prepped you for this life, and he surrounded you with people who would help shape you into who you are supposed to be. In order to understand yourself better, you have to gain some insight into your family's mental and spiritual history in the same way that you would seek information regarding your medical history. When you're able to determine your family legacy, you can break any generational curses or barriers that may be holding you back from your God-given purpose in life.

Determining Your Passion

So what drives you? What gets you out of bed in the morning and looking forward to the day ahead? What stimulates your mind and gets your heart pounding? In other words, what is your passion? What is God's assignment for you? In *God Is My CEO—Following God's Principles in a Bottom-Line World,* author Larry Julian says that "God created each person for specific reasons, tasks, and purposes, and He equipped each one of us with the perfect combination of talents, skills, and abilities required to find fulfillment for our lives." Each of us has a purpose in this life. It may be big or small. It may be something that will affect the lives of millions. Then again, it may be that you were sent here to touch one life in particular. Of course, that is not for you or I to determine.

Passion and Purpose

There is one quality which one must possess to win, and that is DEFINITENESS OF PURPOSE, the knowledge of what one wants, and a burning DESIRE to possess it.
　　—Napoleon Hill, *Think and Grow Rich*

Successful people are fueled by passion. It's what separates them from the herd. When you're passionate about your work, it doesn't really seem like work. In *Leadership GOLD,* John C. Maxwell says that "success is knowing your purpose in life, growing to your maximum potential, and sowing seeds that benefit others." On the other hand, if you're not passionate about what you're doing, you probably won't have much success in it. As Larry Julian says in *God Is My CEO,* "Finding meaning and purpose in our work is the key to both personal fulfillment and professional success."

It's easy to recognize individuals who have a driving passion and a true sense of purpose. Take Amos Yakhoob, for example, one of nine children born into an immigrant family in Deerfield, Michigan, during the early 1900s. Back then money was tight, so, like many kids, Amos was put to work at an early age. He got his first job at the age of ten selling newspapers. A year later he was working as a candy maker at a burlesque theater. Over time, he worked as a busboy and a punch-press operator's assistant. He even worked in a lumber yard for a while, saving pennies as he went, so that he could pursue his dream to be in show business. Finally, he scrounged up enough money to buy a couple suits and some shoes, and he headed off to Detroit, where he landed a job as a singer on *The Happy Hour Club* radio show.

Amos's hard work and determination paid off. In less than a year, he was earning upward of $500 a week—a hefty sum in those days. Soon he became one of the most famous entertainers in the business, landing roles in movies like *The Jazz Singer* (1952) and on nationally broadcast television programs like *The Dick van Dyke Show* and *The Andy Griffith Show.*

Amos, by the way, was his real name. But he's better known as the legendary Danny Thomas.

Thomas had a driving passion that led him to pursue his dreams and his life's purpose. He had other passions as well, one of which was his desire to help sick children.

Back when he was just starting out in show business, Thomas's wife was pregnant with their first child. Not yet established in the industry, he wasn't sure if he should continue pursuing his dream or get a normal job in order to support his family. So he prayed to St. Jude, the patron saint of the hopeless, to help him decide. He even promised to build a shrine to the saint in gratitude for his help. In 1962, Thomas kept his word when he founded the St. Jude Children's Research Hospital in Memphis, Tennessee. Today it's a leading center in the research and treatment of pediatric cancers, and thousands of children from all over the world have been treated there since its inception.

Thomas may have made his fortune and built his persona in show business, but St. Jude's was his greatest accomplishment. Eventually he was recognized for his philanthropic efforts with a papal knighthood by Pope Paul VI and a Congressional Gold Medal from President Ronald Reagan. Not bad for a kid who had come from such meager beginnings.

Thomas's story epitomizes what's possible when you follow your passion, make good use of your talents, and live your life with a sense of purpose. Of course, this is just one example. But it's a powerful illustration of what you can achieve when you follow your passion and live your life every day with the unyielding belief that you were put here for a specific reason, for a God-given purpose.

And make no mistake about it—you were.

Say, like many Americans, you have a passion for football. You can't get enough of it. You live for autumn weekends. You can read defenses like Peyton Manning, and you can name all the Super Bowl MVPs from the last ten years. Good for you. However, that doesn't necessarily mean you were meant to *play* football. If you're five feet four and weigh 140 pounds, chances are you're not going to be drafted by the Pittsburgh Steelers anytime soon.

Does this mean your passion is misguided? Worthless? Not exactly. It just means that you probably weren't meant to *play* football. Maybe you could put your passion to good use as a youth-football coach. Who knows, maybe one day one of your former players could grow up to be a star football player, thanks to the knowledge and passion you shared with him when he was younger.

We all have different passions, things that inspire us and get our hearts racing. Some of these passions, however, may have nothing to do with what your true *purpose* is here on Earth. The trick is to figure out how to pursue your passion in a way that will enable you to fulfill God's *purpose* for you. Determining what stirs your heart is important. But it's essential to discover where your God-given talents truly lie and to use that knowledge to achieve your true purpose.

Greg, for example, has a passion for cycling and would like nothing more than to compete in the Tour de France. But Greg is realistic. Although he enjoys cycling and can hold his own with most of the other riders he knows, he understands that he doesn't have the ability to compete with the world-class riders that complete in the Tour. That's all right, though, because Greg has other passions as well, such as his zeal for business consulting, leadership, and enterprise development. And it's in these passions where his true, God-given talents lie. That's how he has been able to achieve such a high level of success in his career and even build his own leadership-development company. You see, Greg recognized his true talents and skills and put them to use by finding a purpose he could be passionate about: helping other business professionals find success. He was able to come to this conclusion through self-assessment, introspection, prayer, and the trusted advice of his own personal board of directors—his Master Mind.

In "Finding Your Purpose: Identifying Your Strengths and Going for Growth," an article that appeared in the August 5, 2009, issue of *SUCCESS* magazine, John C. Maxwell talks about two "paths" you need to take in order to discover your true purpose in life. One is passion, which he calls "the great energizer." Successful people, says Maxwell, "never run out of energy and they can't wait to get going." But, he cautions, "passion can only get you so far," and it's not always 100 percent accurate. According to Maxwell, what you really need to focus on is your "Strength Zone Path," a phrase he borrowed from Marcus Buckingham's book *Now, Discover Your Strengths.*

What do you do well that sets you apart from other people? Once you determine your Strength Zone Path, or what we like to call your *flow,* you have to fine-tune it and work hard at strengthening and developing it. Then and only then will you be able to set yourself apart from the pack. When you are able to master and stay in your flow, success is inevitable.

So what exactly makes you tick? What are your passions? Your interests? Where do your true talents and skills lie? What is your flow? What is the thing that's unique about you that you need to focus on and develop in order to catch your dreams? These are the types of questions you need to ask yourself in order to determine your true purpose and how to make the most of it.

An easy way to start is by making lists of your goals, passions, and talents. What do you love to do? What do you do really well? What do others say that you are great at? What do you value about yourself? About others? What do you want your legacy to be? These may not be easy questions to answer. But they are absolutely necessary in having a better understanding of your personality.

And don't worry if you can't figure out your purpose right away. It may take years before you discover your true calling. As Larry Julian says, "With patience, we learn to run the race we have been called to run, in spite of the pressure that surrounds us."

Know Thyself

In *The Law of Success in Sixteen Lessons,* Napoleon Hill says, "No man has a chance to enjoy permanent success until he begins to look in a mirror for the real cause of all of his mistakes." In other words, until you really know yourself and achieve "Personal Mastery," you can't get where you want to be in life. Personal Mastery is a heightened self-awareness—a deep understanding of one's own behaviors, motivators, competencies, and shortcomings. It is an understanding of what differentiates you from everyone else.

Self-assessment is hardly a new concept. In fact, it goes all the way back to the fifth and fourth centuries, when Hippocrates (460–370 BC), the noted Greek philosopher and "father of Western medicine," devised his theory of the "four humors." Swiss psychologist Carl Gustav Jung (1875–1961) built on Hippocrates's model when in 1921 he published his *Psychological Types*, in which he described eight distinct personality types. Then, in 1962, Katharine Cook Briggs and her daughter, Isabel Briggs Myers, built on Jung's model with what would become known as the Myers-Briggs Type Indicator (MBTI). The MBTI assessment was designed to "measure psychological preferences in how people perceive the world and make decisions."

Although each is different and none is 100 percent foolproof, self-assessments can still be valuable in helping you create a clearer picture of who you are and what makes you tick. They can build a foundation for self-understanding on which you can build and grow. When you understand your unique makeup—your passions, your talents, and even your weaknesses—you're better equipped to interact with others in a positive way and to react to different circumstances you encounter. The point isn't to label you; it's to help you understand what type of person you are, where you excel, where you may need work, and how you prefer to communicate with others. And when you know these things, you have a better understanding of who you really are, which is one of the core principles of the Spider Web Philosophy.

Ellen Langas, president of NouSoma Communications Inc. (nousoma.com) and author of The Girls Know How® series (girlsnowhow.com), learned the value of self-assessment early in her career, when she discovered that people generally saw her as a more confident, outgoing, and successful individual that she considered herself to be. "It helped me realize that I was selling myself short when it came to self-confidence," she says. "It gave me a boost in the right direction."

Langas believes that personality assessments are a valuable tool that can help you compare how others' perceptions of you may differ from your own. "A person's perception about you is their reality, so it's important that people know the real you. If you don't offer insight into your capabilities and dreams, you can't expect that they will register on anyone's radar."

In the previous chapter, we talked about the importance of authenticity when building your relationships. However, we didn't mention that there is both outward and inward authenticity. Authentic relationships rise out of you being the authentic you. In order to discover your authentic you, you need to be wholly self-aware of your talents and passions.

LaRae Quy knows about authenticity. She was with the FBI for twenty-five years as an undercover counterintelligence agent working to expose foreign spies. On her blog (laraequy.com) she uses her FBI knowledge and experience to teach people how to "cope with the unexpected and think on your feet so you can bring out the best in yourself and others."

In a guest post on Michael Hyatt's blog (michaelhyatt.com) entitled "5 Ways to Become a More Authentic Leader," Quy touches on the importance of knowing yourself. "Leadership begins with knowing who you are and what you believe," she writes. "Authenticity is the need for leaders to be themselves regardless of the situation. For this reason, it is more than self-awareness. It is the ability to share the deepest and truest part of ourselves with others."

Quy says that, while it's helpful to watch and learn from others, the truly successful leaders are those who embrace the journey of self-discovery. "Self-awareness makes it easier to us to view our choices through a lens that brings our values into focus. If we are self-aware, we can begin to understand how well our actions align with our beliefs, values, strengths and weaknesses."

Take some time and have fun with self-assessments. See if they don't shed some light on who you really are. Use the results to identify your weaker personality traits, and then consider how you can eliminate them or maybe work on them in order to strengthen your ability to interact and connect with others. Share the results of your test with your closest friends and those you look to for advice, and ask them to work with you to develop a plan of action for personal growth. Each member of our group has taken various self-assessments and shared the results with the other members for evaluation and feedback. Doing so enabled us to get honest feedback on the accuracy and validity of the test results, as well as advice on how to best use the results in order to grow and develop as individuals.

Of course, taking the necessary steps to discover your true self is one thing; accepting the results is another thing altogether. Sometimes it can be hard to look at yourself in the mirror. But if you ever want to get what you want out of this life, it's imperative that you do so. Just remember, when you show yourself who you are or are not—believe it!

Chapter 2 Takeaways
So let's review:

- The type of web you need depends on who you really are and what you're trying to catch.
- You are unique. Your web must also be unique.
- Each of us has our own set of God-given skills and talents that we need to identify and put to good use.
- Each of us has at least one passion, one driving force that excites us in a way nothing else can. Recognize this passion, harness it, and use it to help you achieve your true purpose.
- One of the most important factors in achieving success and fulfillment in life is a sense of self-awareness and how you prefer to interact with others.
- Inward authenticity is just as important as outward authenticity.
- Once you perform a self-assessment, share the outcome with your closest friends in order to get honest advice on how to best take advantage of your uniqueness to develop and grow.
- When you show yourself who you are or who you are not—believe it!
- There may be more than one authentic version of you.

Worksheet #2

What is your brand? What makes you unique? What are your defining characteristics?

What are your natural talents?

What are you passionate about?

What do others say that you are great at?

How do you think others perceive you?

How different is your professional persona from your "home" or personal persona?

Is there a difference because you are not working in a field that allows you to be the "real" you, or are you a complex individual who's personal and professional passion and purpose make it necessary to be very different in these different settings?

Chapter 3

STRATEGIC WEB CONSTRUCTION –
Placement, Silk Selection, Timing, and Faith:

CREATING YOUR NETWORK

I f you've ever had the privilege of watching a construction project, you know what an amazing feat it is. It's an incredibly complicated process with hundreds of intricate steps, each of which has to be taken in a specific order. Depending on the scale of the project, it can take months or even years to complete.

Now imagine another type of construction project. One that's just as complicated and intricate, with each part serving a unique and essential purpose. That's exactly what an orb-web spider does almost every day.

Using its own body as a measuring stick, the spider first lets out a line of silk and allows the wind to carry it across the gap. Once this sticky line is in place, the spider reinforces it with another thread. The spider repeats this again and again until this anchor line is strong enough to support the rest of the web. From there, the spider goes on to lay the radials and the circular core of the web, working from the center outward, and then back to the center again as it lays the adhesive line that will ensnare its prey.

The process of creating your own web can be just as elaborate and beautiful. It's just going to take a little more time. In order for it to catch your dreams and aspirations, your web must be more than a random selection of people from your life. It must be custom designed, systematically and with purpose. And when you dedicate yourself to your web, when you grow it over time and continually work to strengthen and maintain it, the rewards will prove it was all worthwhile.

Strategically Placing Your Web

When a spider picks a location for its web, it puts it in a spot where it's most likely to catch something. If, over time, the web doesn't yield the desired results, the spider must tear it down and rebuild the web in a place where it will be more successful.

The same goes for you. You may already have a web. Most people do. But if your current web is not working out for you, if it's not getting you where you want to be, you need to consider if it is "placed" correctly. In other words, you have to have the right types of connections. This is extremely important. If your web is not placed correctly, you could end up destroying the very fabric that you are investing in.

But how exactly do you find the types of connections you need in order to achieve your desired goal? Well, a lot of that depends on the goal itself. If you're looking to grow your local sales numbers, connecting with someone across the country might not do anything for you. Likewise, if you're looking to strengthen your marriage, it probably won't help you to connect with someone who's been married and divorced three times. Determine what exactly you're trying to catch, and then figure out what types of connections best support you in this endeavor.

Let's say there's this girl named Susie whose passions are cooking and writing. More than anything, Susie would love to have a weekly or monthly column in a magazine, where she could write about all her adventures—and misadventures—in the kitchen. So she begins her own cooking blog and starts to build her web of readers, slowly but surely, hoping that one day she'll have a big enough following that some editor will take notice and offer her a job. In the meantime Susie starts to connect with anyone and everyone she comes across. She hands out her custom-designed business cards everywhere she goes. She e-mails all her friends and relatives to tell them about her blog. She blasts her posts out to her Facebook friends and Twitter followers. For a while, Susie notices that the number of visitors and subscribers to her cooking blog is steadily climbing. But then, gradually, the numbers begin to level off, and the number of weekly visitors declines.

What happened? How did Susie lose the momentum that was steadily growing her web? In this hypothetical situation, the problem wasn't the way Susie was working on expanding her web. The problem was that she wasn't *placing* it correctly. Sure, she may have been able to get her friends and family and some other random connections to check out her blog and even stick around for a post or two. But once the novelty wore off, many of her visitors just faded away. They weren't interested in Susie and her blog for its subject. They were just visiting because they were acquainted with her and because she asked them to do so. Once they fulfilled that obligation, in their minds, they no longer had a reason to return. As a result, Susie's blog became ineffective in helping her accomplish her chief aim—landing a weekly magazine column.

Now let's imagine that Susie recognizes her mistake—that her web wasn't placed correctly—and decides to start over, this time with a more finely tuned focus. This time, instead of just making connections willy-nilly, Susie does her research and finds people and groups with a specific interest in cooking. She contacts these people directly and lets them know about her blog. Then she starts attending cooking shows and conventions, handing out her business cards and striking up conversations with the people she meets. She goes online and finds other cooking bloggers and asks to do guest posts on their blogs. She also finds online cooking groups and chat rooms, where she can speak with others in the field and continue to build her credibility. Then, once she's developed a respectable following and some credibility, both locally in her hometown and online, she begins to send out queries to the editors of her favorite cooking magazines. Finally, through perseverance and hard work, Susie is rewarded when she receives a call from an editor who discovered her blog through a colleague in the cooking field and says she wants Susie to write for their magazine!

So, OK, this is just a hypothetical situation, and happy endings are never guaranteed. But the lesson here is real. When Susie's web was made up of the wrong types of connections, when it was "placed" incorrectly, her web was ineffective and unable to catch her desired goal. On the other hand, when her web was placed correctly, when she focused on building it with the right types of connections—people in the cooking world—Susie's web was able to catch opportunity when it came flying by.

Take a look at your web. Is it placed correctly for the type of opportunity or aspiration you're trying to catch? If not, figure out what you can do to make sure that it is strategically placed in order to get you where you want to be.

What Type of Silk Do You Have?

Spiders produce different types of silk for different purposes. One type is used for the web's "spokes" and for an emergency lifeline. Then there's the sticky kind that ensnares the prey. Another type of silk is used for making protective egg sacs or retreats, and yet another is used to secure anything that gets caught in the web.

When it comes to you and your web, think of your relationships as your "silk." You have all different types of relationships, and each has a unique and important purpose. When you're building your web, you need to analyze your various relationships and determine which ones are beneficial to you and can help get you where you want to be. Your work relationships may be valuable to your career, but can they help you with your love life? Then again, your friendships may provide the emotional support you need, but can they really help you build your career?

Strength, stickiness, and elasticity are the three primary properties of spider silk. When we're talking about your own personal web, the highest-quality silk is that with the greatest mixture of these three properties. By *strength* we mean how much you can depend on the person to provide the type of support you need. *Stickiness* is another way of saying reliability—how much you can depend on that person to be there for you and stick with you through the tough times. When we're talking about *elasticity*, we mean flexibility—that is, the connection's ability to adapt to changing situations and still remain strong and reliable.

Your Master Mind should be made of this type of high-quality silk. Then, as you build outward, you should determine what the perceived value of every relationship is. Some may be more elastic; others may be stickier or stronger than the rest. Once you identify the value of each of your relationships, make the most of it, and maintain it accordingly.

When you're spinning your web, you have to be able to evaluate each of your relationships objectively and then determine if they are truly helping you get where you want to be in life. If a relationship is toxic or negative, it can prevent you from growing as a person and achieving your true purpose. Therefore, it may have to be eliminated from your life altogether. Does this mean you have to cut ties with every person who's not helping you reach a specific goal in your life? Certainly not. We all have casual relationships—those that we cherish but maybe aren't as strong or as sticky as the others. But when it comes to building your web, the one that you will use to catch your dreams and ambitions, you must be sure that it's made up of authentic relationships, ones that have a vested interest in you and your God-given purpose. Otherwise it will be weak, misplaced, and ultimately ineffective.

One of the most difficult things you may have to do through this process is decide whether or not a family member is of the highest-grade silk. It could be a parent, a sibling, or even your spouse. Unfortunately, sometimes in life, those who love us most can end up doing the most damage. These types of relationships have a stickiness quality solely because of your genetic connection to them, but they may be lacking in strength and elasticity. In other words, they might not be strong or flexible enough to provide the type of support you need. Your family members may believe that their intentions are in your best interest, but in reality they may end up doing more harm than good.

Dysfunction exists in every family on one level or another. It's the depth of that dysfunction that differs from family to family. If you're not careful, it can derail you and prevent you from obtaining your objectives. Sometimes our parents can project on us the dreams and goals that they were unable to achieve themselves. They see their children as an opportunity to correct the mistakes that they made along the way. Because of this, parents may try to guide their children in a certain direction that may not be right for them and what their God-given assignment is for this life. This isn't always done consciously or maliciously, but it happens. Recognize what's right for you, and don't allow yourself to be influenced by faulty guidance, no matter whom it comes from.

Timing Is Everything

For decades, scientists have been trying unsuccessfully to replicate spider silk. They are, however, getting closer every day to unlocking the secrets that give silk its incredible strength and elasticity. According to a 2006 article by Lee Dye, written for ABCNews.com, we've been able to identify the key proteins used by spiders and silkworms to make their silk, but we haven't been able to translate this information into a mass-produced, ultra-strong, synthetic silk product. That is, until recently, when scientists made a breakthrough discovery: *it's all in the timing.*

David Kaplan, professor and chair of biomedical engineering at Tufts University near Boston, along with his former postdoctoral fellow, Hyoung-Joon Jin, determined that spiders are able to prevent the silk's proteins from crystallizing until they are ready for spinning. Until humans can figure out how to do the same in the lab, we won't be able to recreate the same strength-and-flexibility combination in our synthetic silk that Mother Nature does in hers.

It's all in the timing. That's great. But how does this translate to you and your efforts in building your own web?

Let's consider Dwight. As a management consultant in the aviation and construction industry, Dwight specializes in major billion-dollar development programs. Back in 2009 he was in Abu Dhabi managing the expansion of their international airport. Prior to that, he was in Atlanta managing a billion-dollar airport-development program at the busiest airport in the world. In 2010, he was given the opportunity to relocate to Denver, where he would oversee the airport's South Terminal Redevelopment Program. So, he and his family packed up and moved to the "Mile-High City" to start another chapter of their life together and take on their next life assignment.

That next spring, Dwight was attending an aviation conference when he was introduced to this engineering executive, who told Dwight that he'd like to have dinner with him sometime. Understanding the value of connections, even when it's one of your competitors, Dwight agreed to the meeting, expecting nothing more than a nice meal with an industry colleague.

During this meeting the man and Dwight really hit it off. They realized that they shared many of the same industry connections, and both talked about how much they enjoyed the leadership aspect of the business. That's when the man dropped a bombshell. He told Dwight that he had had his résumé for months, and he'd been wanting to have a conversation with him for some time now. He also wanted Dwight to meet with his company's upper management. Dwight had no idea how this gentleman had come across his résumé in the first place, and he was more than intrigued. So he decided to take the man up on his offer.

Over the next several weeks, Dwight met with many of the upper-level executives of this multi-billion-dollar organization. He even met with the CEO, who, after a brief conversation, asked Dwight what he really wanted to know about the company. Dwight was satisfied in his current position, and he knew that he had nothing to lose, so his answer was honest: "I'd like to know if I have a shot at your job as CEO."

Three weeks later Dwight's phone rang. It was his business colleague from the dinner meeting, and he had a message for Dwight: "We want you."

So how did this happen? How did an innocent dinner meeting turn into an incredible job offer that brought Dwight even closer to his dream of becoming a CEO? Plain and simple—it was all in the timing. Dwight leveraged the power and influence of his web and the strong connections he had built over time in order to catch his dream job. A couple of years earlier, another major competitor had approached Dwight with a job offer. But it just wasn't the right time for him. He had just moved to Denver from Abu Dhabi, and he didn't want to uproot his wife and kids again so soon. So he declined the offer. Did he regret the decision? No, but he wondered if maybe he had passed up a good opportunity. Then he received this new offer, which was much better and would allow him and his family to remain in Denver while he continued to build his career. *It's all in the timing and placement of your web, not the chasing of your dreams.*

Dwight's résumé was impressive, no doubt. But his qualifications alone didn't make that company search him out and bend over backward to get him to join their team. Somewhere along the line, thanks to his high moral character, strong work ethic, and, most important, his extensive and well-maintained web, someone who respected Dwight and held him in high regard recommended and vouched for him. Dwight didn't have to go out and pursue opportunity. Instead he worked hard, built solid relationships, and maintained them, and as a result, opportunity came looking for him.

Faith

God seems to throw Himself on the side of the man who knows exactly what he wants, if he is determined to get just that!
—Napoleon Hill

Spinning a solid, well-placed, effective web that will catch what you're looking for is an intricate and time-consuming process. It takes skill, focus, and steadfast determination.

But even that's not enough. No matter how meticulous, focused, and dedicated you are, there is still one more ingredient you need in order to build the perfect web for you: God.

How can you look at a spider web and not believe in God? The beauty, the complexity, the innovative design—it's a miracle of nature, really. A spider does its best to build a dependable web, using the resources and skills that nature—God—has provided it. But once the web spinning is complete, the spider must be patient and have *faith* that the insects will come. The spider puts in the time and effort; God brings the just rewards.

"Faith," said Napoleon Hill, "is the 'eternal elixir' which gives life, power, and action to the impulse of thought!" It is "the basis of all 'miracles,' and all mysteries which cannot be analyzed by the rules of science!" Faith, particularly your faith in God, is a huge part of the Spider Web Philosophy. In fact, when you're trying to catch opportunities and achieve the life you've always wanted, nothing is more important than your faith in the Divine. Overall, the Spider Web Philosophy is more a method than a solution. However, it is a solution in the same way that Christ is a solution. He is the conduit, the means to everlasting life. The Spider Web Philosophy is the conduit to catching what you want out of life, to taking you to the next level. Only once you've done your part and put in the time and effort to build your web will God bring the opportunities to it. Once you build your web, the rest is out of your hands. And honestly, that's the way it should be. As Larry Julian writes in *God Is My CEO—Following God's Principles in a Bottom-Line World,* "surrendering control to God is a better plan than trying to take charge of things beyond our control."

Nothing happens by chance. Our paths are divinely ordained and orchestrated. God allows us to choose and, if we submit, will order our steps for us. God will always bring peace to your life when you choose to submit your life to him, and there is no better feeling of peace than being in the perfect will for your life. No one in our webs came to us by accident. They were all brought to us by divine assignment. Once you set your mind on what you're trying to catch, God will put all the relationships you need in your path.

We are much more than just a title, a name, or an occupation. We are spirit beings, each with a unique and important purpose—a God-given assignment. All of us have an assignment the day we are born. You have to listen attentively and be willing to walk boldly and courageously in your assignment. After all, it is God's instruction for your life. Everything and everyone on Earth, all of God's creation, contains an instruction, an assignment, to serve a different purpose. Within everything created is a desire and command to increase, produce, and multiply. Inside each one of us is an invisible calling.

In life, God provides us with opportunities to hear and obey. Before Dwight left for Abu Dhabi, he and his wife, Eleanore, spent months meditating, praying, researching, analyzing, and testing this opportunity. After having spent twelve years at World Changers Church International and seven years overseeing the engineering and construction of the "Most Important Runway in the World" at the busiest airport in the world, Hartsfield-Jackson Atlanta International Airport, Dwight knew that it was not by accident that he was chosen to lead in this industry.

The years Dwight put in and the experiences he gained exposed him to a new way of thinking. He now had a global perspective, and it was clear to him that God had equipped him and prepared him for his purpose, his divine assignment. When accepting this assignment to go to Abu Dhabi in the United Arab Emirates and work on the new airport there, Dwight was submitting to God all that he was and had. He had just built a new house in Atlanta, and he and Eleanore had kids to think about, too. But they always agreed that they would open their hearts and minds to receive what God had planned for them, even if it meant they'd have to face challenges and discomfort as a family. What they've found is that most times it does mean leaving a place of familiarity and comfort, but in the end, it always leads to growth. The Middle East was certainly out of Dwight's comfort zone and that of his family. But when God wants to broaden your perspective, it takes stepping away to see from his perspective, which is a truly global perspective.

As William Jennings Bryan once said, "Destiny is not a matter of chance, it is a matter of choice; it is not a thing to be waited for, it is a thing to be achieved." For Dwight, going to Abu Dhabi was about accepting an assignment, an instruction, a dream, a passion, and a destiny.

It was an amazing experience that they never would have had if they had not put their faith and trust in God. The relationships that Dwight created, the people who he and his family met—people from the Sudan, Finland, Germany, Syria, and Egypt, as well as the United States—would become their friends for life.

We are all created to solve a problem, and we are compensated based on the problems we solve. You need to pinpoint exactly what it is that you do for others. What problems have you solved for others? Make your chief aim to help people. Get the person you work for promoted. That person may never acknowledge you, but he or she isn't the one who's going to thank you—it's *God* who's going to help you. At the end of the day, if you keep working hard, God will reward you. It may take a hundred failures to finally figure out what works. Just look at Thomas Edison.

Chapter 3 Takeaways

So let's review:

- In order to catch what you want, your web must be custom designed, systematically and with purpose.
- You have to strategically place your web where it needs to be in order for it to be most effective for you—that is, you have to select the right connections based on what you are trying to catch.
- You have to be able to objectively look at each of your relationships and determine if they are truly helping you get where you want to be in life.
- It's all in the timing. When you make the right kinds of connections and foster strong relationships, good things will come to you—in God's time.
- Only once you've done your part and put in the time and effort to build your web, God will bring the opportunities to it.

Worksheet #3

What networks do you currently belong to?

List your five closest relationships.

Of all your current relationships, which ones do you think can help you capture your goals?

Write about a time in your life when the timing of a relationship (personal and/or professional) just wasn't right.

If you don't believe in God, then what are you willing to identify as "bigger" than you (karma, the greater good, a sense of morality) that will not only hold you accountable, but also allow you to trust that those things you cannot control will still work out in your favor?

Chapter 4

THE WEB'S CORE -
*A Place to Rest,
Replenish, and
Receive:*

YOUR MASTER
MIND

Envision the spider web, spanning a void, radiating outward from the center to its various connection points. And on that center, that core, sits the spider—poised, focused, and ready. There the spider remains, at the web's strongest point, conserving its energy while it patiently waits for an insect to fly into its silken trap. It's here in the center where the web's strength and stability lies. It's here where the spider is in the best position to catch its prey.

When you think about your own web and what you'd like to catch, it's just as important that you have a strong center to serve as a foundation. You need to have a secure place where you can rest, replenish your energy, and be suitably placed so that you're ready and able to catch the opportunities that come your way. This center, this core, is your Master Mind.

The Master Mind is the ultimate form of focused collaboration. It not only generates new ideas; it unlocks them. An idea may already be inside you, waiting to be born; the Master Mind can help to bring it out. It helps you stay focused. It keeps your attention on your intention, and it makes sure that you're always ready to catch the opportunities that come your way.

The Master Mind

The Master Mind concept was first introduced by Napoleon Hill, who coined the term after interviewing more than five hundred American millionaires over a span of nearly twenty years. These great minds and captains of industry, men like Henry Ford, John D. Rockefeller, Thomas Edison, and Andrew Carnegie, who commissioned Hill's work, all utilized this powerful concept to help them achieve amazing levels of success and financial wealth. The term itself was taken directly from Hill's interview with Carnegie, in which Carnegie said, "If you wish to know how I got my money—if that is what you call success—I will answer your question by saying that we have a master mind here in our business, and that mind is made up of more than a score of men who constitute my personal staff of superintendents and managers and accountants and chemists and other necessary types." Carnegie's own Master Mind group was made up of around fifty men who he felt could help him in the achievement of one definite purpose: making and selling his steel. Carnegie said that it was the "sum total of the minds in the group, coordinated, organized and directed to a definite end in a spirit of harmonious cooperation" that helped him find such enormous financial success.

In *The Law of Success in Sixteen Lessons* (1925), Hill defined the "Master Mind" as "the harmonious cooperation of two or more people who ally themselves for the purpose of accomplishing any given task." When he penned his guide to success, *Think and Grow Rich,* in 1937, the Master Mind was one of the thirteen principles Hill cited that could help you realize your dreams and elevate your chances for financial success. He also refined the definition of the concept as the "coordination of knowledge and effort in a spirit of harmony between two or more people for the attainment of a definite purpose." To put it in basic terms, it's the process of bringing individuals together in order to cultivate new ideas and to facilitate success and achievement.

Hill believed that when people come together through the Master Mind concept, magical things happen. "The human mind is a form of energy, a part of it being spiritual in nature," he said. And when two or more minds came together in a "spirit of harmony," the energy from each mind joins to form what he referred to as the "collective of the mind." According to Hill, "each person in the group becomes vested with the power to contact with and gather knowledge through the 'subconscious' minds of all the other members of the group." This then stimulates each of the members' minds to "a higher rate of vibration," which fosters new ideas and gives each member access to a "sixth sense."

The Master Mind concept is just as relevant today as it was in Hill's time. There are literally thousands of these groups across the country, each with its own unique purpose and variation on the concept. Just google "Master Mind group," and you'll see what we mean.

Napoleon Hill once said that "more gold has been mined from the thoughts of men than has been taken from the earth." If you want to get to the next level, you have to be able to harness the power of imagination. You have to be able to develop new ideas. When you come together with others, each of you brings a unique set of ideas to the table. The harmonious energy of the Master Mind group identifies these ideas and opens the way for new ones. It unlocks the ideas that are within each member and helps you develop them and put them to use.

One of the Napoleon Hill Foundation's declared values is "Collaboration is essential to create miracles." When people put their heads together toward a common purpose, great things can happen. You can be the smartest person in the world, but unless you are willing to accept the ideas of others and learn from them, there is no guarantee that you will reach your full potential. As Hill points out in *The Law of Success in Sixteen Lessons*, with knowledge comes power—potential power. Power itself, he says, is "organized knowledge, expressed through intelligent efforts." The Master Mind concept puts this principle into action. It helps you organize your ideas and use this combined power to help you achieve your goals.

Your Master Mind group is your personal board of directors. Collectively, your objectives are to help the other members discover their true selves, help them find success, and help them achieve their greater purposes in life. As a member of this group, each of you has a responsibility to learn everything you can about the other members—their goals, dreams, personality traits, weaknesses, fears, and so on—and then use that information to provide sound advice and guidance. It is the core of your web, the foundation around which the rest of your web is built. It is the place where you can come to rest, recuperate, and meditate, while you wait for opportunity to come to you. It is where your success begins.

In *Leadership Gold: Lessons I've Learned from a Lifetime of Leading*, John C. Maxwell writes that "success is compounded when others join our cause." The Master Mind puts this theory into action, recruiting other like-minded individuals to "join our cause" and help us get what we want out of life. It is centered on the idea of accountability. In his book, Maxwell touches on the importance of accountability in getting you where you want to be. "The willingness to seek and accept advice is a great indicator of accountability," he writes. "If you seek it early—before you take action—you will be less likely to get off track. Most wrong actions come about because people are not being held accountable early enough." In other words, you can have all the best intentions in the world, but if there's no one there to hold you accountable, to make sure that you follow through with your intentions, your chances of success are slim to none.

Maxwell doesn't take the act of giving advice lightly either. For him the person who gives advice has a responsibility to hold the recipient accountable. "It is my business as the influencer to know their business and makes sure my investment is wise," he writes. "To do that, I periodically check up on them to make sure the 'transaction' was a wise one and that it is paying off."

You don't have to look any further than our own Master Mind group to understand the power of this amazing tool. Before we started harnessing the power of the Master Mind concept, each of us already belonged to some type of network. We had our families, our friends, our civic engagement, our religious involvement, and so on. We had our coworkers and other business colleagues, and each of us took part in different forms of social media. Each of these groups had a particular strength and usefulness, but none could match the collective power we generated when we embraced Hill's ideology. When we finally came together and followed this proven model, our understanding of ourselves—and in turn, the level of our success—reached an entirely new and exciting level.

While other Master Minds may be focused on one particular thing—financial success, romance, spirituality, and so on—ours is more about life in general. It's about becoming better human beings. We strive to keep each other on the right path toward our specific goals and dreams. We also share similar values, and more importantly, we agree on the prioritization of those values. As a result, our Master Mind has become an invaluable tool for helping us figure out who we are, what we want to get out of this life, and how to get it.

Establishing a Master Mind group is one of the main attributes of the Spider Web Philosophy. It's an essential tool in realizing and catching your aspirations. Can you achieve success without it? Maybe. But when you invest in a Master Mind group and learn to tap into its intrinsic power, you multiply your chances of success exponentially, regardless of your endeavor.

Creating Your Master Mind Group

When you decide to form your own Master Mind group, you need to put some serious thought into it. Remember, this is the core of your web—the foundation. If the foundation is weak, it will compromise the strength and effectiveness of the rest of your web as you build it outward.

You must use only the highest grade of silk in your core. In other words, the members of your Master Mind must be your most authentic relationships. You must be meticulous in the selection process and be sure that the other members of your group are committed to personal growth and development, not only for themselves but for every other member of the group. Your Master Mind group is as close to the covenant relationship of holy matrimony as you can get. Therefore, you have to treat it with the level of respect and attention that it deserves.

When you're considering potential members for your Master Mind group, you should keep certain factors in mind:

Diversity of opinion—Being in a group where everyone thinks alike won't do you any good. You have to surround yourself with people who you respect but do not necessarily always agree with. Avoid confrontational people, but embrace diversity of opinion. Disagreement, after all, can be a good thing. It challenges you and forces you to look at things from different points of view. And if you wish to achieve greater success and fulfillment in life, you need to be consistently challenged and pushed beyond what you thought were your limits. Growth comes from stretching, discomfort, and tension. Think about when you exercise. If you never challenge yourself, you'll only see limited results. But when you push yourself to lift a little more or run that extra mile, it makes your muscles grow in order to compensate. The same goes for your emotional and psychological growth. The more you are challenged by other points of view and opinions, the easier it will be for you to see things in a new light.

Trust—How well do you actually know this person that you're considering for your Master Mind group? How well does he or she know you? Can you trust him or her to be honest with you and to provide honest feedback? Can you trust yourself to be totally open and honest with the person about you and every aspect of your life? Can you trust the person to take this process seriously? Can you trust him or her to really listen to you, give careful consideration to your needs and desires, and then give an honest effort to do what he or she can to help you achieve your aspirations? If the answer to any of these questions is no, then you may want to look elsewhere. Full transparency is paramount to this relationship.

You must also trust in yourself. Trust your intuition, and listen to what your heart says about the potential partner. Sometimes our innermost feelings can tell us all we really need to know and can help us make the right decisions in life. Listen to your heart, and trust in it.

Motivation—Does the potential member share the same level of motivation as you when it comes to achieving success and happiness? Does he or she share a driving passion for personal growth and understanding? Does he or she truly believe that everyone has a God-given purpose? Does the potential member live his or her life as a conduit through which blessings flow or rather as a container waiting to be filled? These are all important factors in your group's effectiveness. And if the motivation is lacking, your Master Mind group will be weak as a result.

Dependability—How dependable is the person you're considering for your group? Can you rely on him or her to be committed to the group and its vision? Can you depend on him or her to be at every meeting or call in to your teleconference on time? Will this person be there for you one, five, even ten years down the road, however long the process may take? The members of your Master Mind not only have to be willing; they have to be able as well.

Résumé—What does this individual bring to the table? What unique talents, skills, ideas, and connections does he or she have that will help get you where you want to be? The members of your Master Mind group don't have to be geniuses or millionaires (although it doesn't hurt), but they do need to bring something of value to the table; otherwise they're just dead weight and will drain energy from the other members.

These are just a few things to consider when you're organizing your Master Mind group. The key is to join up with people who share your vision, values, enthusiasm, and commitment to take your life to the next level and achieve success and fulfillment in all your endeavors.

Keeping Your Master Mind Strong
Deciding to form a Master Mind group is one thing; keeping it viable and strong is another. Anyone can form a group with friends and colleagues and

have the best intentions of meeting regularly. But without some agreed-upon guidelines, your group can quickly lose its value to you and the other members' lives.

When the four of us decided to start meeting regularly as a Master Mind group, we agreed on several rules to keep us accountable and ensure we were getting the most out of the process. Since we all live in different parts of the country and at times in different parts of the world, our weekly meetings are held over the phone. We talk once a week, on the same day and at the same time, for a minimum of one hour. Each of us serves as moderator for a month and leads the calls, opening with a prayer and offering some words of inspiration and encouragement. Also, once a month, each person has the opportunity to be the focus of the entire call and present a problem, challenge, or idea to the group for approximately half an hour, with the remaining time set aside for feedback from the group. While we respect the time frames, we always agree to give more time when necessary. The member who is the focus of the call often e-mails reference materials ahead of time for us to review before or during the call. Sometimes a particular subject requires more than one call, and we continue the discussion or follow up with updates the next week.

If at any time a member needs to be excused from a call, that member informs the group ahead of time, and the call proceeds, as long as there are at least three members present. Every call is recorded, and the absent member is expected to listen to the recording and offer feedback at a later date, either by phone or by e-mail. We have also had instances where a member needs to speak to each of the others one-on-one because of time constraints and scheduling conflicts.

Full disclosure is an absolute must in any Master Mind group. Half-truths and partial stories are of no value to anyone. And it works in both directions. Each member needs to provide full disclosure, and the others need to offer completely uncensored, honest opinions; otherwise the entire process is a waste of everyone's time. Because of this, you will have to limit the membership of your Master Mind group. Others have asked to participate in our group, but the amount of openness we share is not appropriate for everyone. We never take things personally or as attacks, even when the feedback is a little harsh. This type of frankness and honesty isn't for everyone. And although our spouses and families get a direct benefit from our involvement in the group, what is said between us stays between us, with limited exceptions. In other words, what happens in the Master Mind stays in the Master Mind.

The four of us also participate in periodic retreats so that we can share time together in a relaxed setting and take advantage of some restful downtime. Some of our most powerful revelations and advice have come during our unstructured recreational time together. And quite frankly, that is often the best time to share with one another, because the relaxed atmosphere allows us to share more freely.

Our Master Mind plan is a solid one, but sticking to it isn't always easy. Each of us lives in a different time zone and has different responsibilities. We have busy travel schedules. Some of us have kids. One of the biggest challenges we've faced has been working on writing this book without losing sight of what we need to give to each other through our original agreed-upon process.

Our Master Mind group isn't perfect. Far from it. But each of us does our best to stay dedicated to the process and the guidelines we agreed on at the beginning. Because of our dedication to the group and our commitment to each other, we've all benefited greatly from our weekly calls, and they are something we have come to look forward to.

Just remember, in order for this process to work for you, you have to put the best interests of the others in front of your own needs and desires. The true power of the Master Mind comes from the collective power of all of the members giving wholly of themselves for the betterment of the others. And when you focus on what you can offer the others, the reward comes back to you tenfold.

Enemies of the Master Mind

If a spider uses weak silk to create the core of its web, the entire web's strength and effectiveness will be compromised. The same can be said for your Master Mind group. No matter how well you plan out the format and process of your group, there are still things you need to watch out for that can undermine your group and diminish its usefulness:

Dishonesty—One of the key components of the Master Mind group is transparency. We cannot stress that point enough. In order for your group's members to be able to truly understand you and provide honest, valuable feedback, you have to be 100 percent honest about your feelings, desires, fears, and goals. The Master Mind group allows you to achieve this level of vulnerability without the fear of embarrassing yourself or offending the other members. You have to be completely honest with yourself and with the other members of your Master Mind group in order for it to be effective. Otherwise you just get tangled up in a web of falsehoods that keep you from catching opportunities. "Seek the counsel of men who will tell you the truth about yourself," said Hill, "even if it hurts you to hear it. Mere commendation will not bring the improvement." In your Master Mind group, just as in life, honesty is always the best policy.

Negativity—Being realistic is one thing. But when you or your colleagues come into the Master Mind with a negative attitude, it can undermine the entire process. Just one negative mind can sabotage the entire group.

Consider Jesus and his Apostles as a Master Mind group. Napoleon Hill noted how many believe that Christ actually discovered the power of "mind chemistry," and that his miracles were made possible through the power that resulted "through the blending of the minds of His twelve disciples." When they were all one harmonious unit, following in the teachings of Christ, they were unstoppable. But when Judas Iscariot decided to break away and betray Jesus, the group lost its collective power. It ceased to exist, and, as Hill wrote, "Jesus met with the supreme catastrophe of His life."

Of course, this was all by divine design and therefore could not be avoided. You, on the other hand, have the power to avoid a similar breakdown in your own Master Mind group by choosing to eliminate negativity within yourself and within the other members of the group. Focus on the positive, and positive things will follow.

Selfishness—Dr. Martin Luther King Jr. once said: "An individual has not begun to live until he can rise above the narrow horizons of his particular individualistic concerns to the broader concerns of all humanity. Every person must decide, at some point, whether they will walk in the light of creative altruism or in the darkness of destructive selfishness." It's human nature to want to help yourself. You want to achieve success and happiness in your life; otherwise you wouldn't be reading this book. However, if you want your Master Mind to be effective and help all members of the group, including yourself, you have to be careful to avoid selfishness. The Bible teaches us to do unto others as we would have done to us. In your Master Mind group, you want the other members to give you their full attention and offer sound advice, without being distracted by their own interests. So shouldn't you do the same for them? Think of others first, and they'll do the same for you.

Being judgmental—Ridicule and judgment have no place in your Master Mind group. Sometimes a decision that one member of the group makes doesn't line up with the consensus of the group. That's just how it is. For example, there have been times when our group provided advice to a member, but that member chose not to follow the advice, and as a result, he faced repercussions. Whenever this happens, it's never right to judge that person and say, "I told you so!" Remember, as a member of a Master Mind, it's not your responsibility to be the judge and jury. Each member of the Master Mind trusts the group to provide positive and honest support and guidance. Whether or not members choose to accept that guidance is up to them. It's up to you to help pick them up when they fall.

Independent of a Master Mind group, it's possible that you *could* be successful, and you *could* find fulfillment and happiness. However, practicing the Master Mind concept exponentially increases your chances of success. It becomes your web's core and foundation. With multiple people helping you with your goals, problems, and ideas, you get the benefit of multiple points of view and opinions, which can be invaluable. Sometimes we just can't see the solution, even when we're looking right at the answer. Sometimes it takes others to see the answer for us.

Our Master Mind group was what generated the idea of the Spider Web Philosophy. It helped us develop and discover this unique way of thinking that has helped us all find a level of success and fulfillment in our lives. Could we have achieved this on our own? Possibly. But then it would've been more luck than anything. When you're part of a Master Mind, you don't have to depend on luck; you can depend on each other.

Chapter 4 Takeaways

So let's review:

- The Master Mind is your web's core. It's where you can rest, reenergize, and be ready to catch the opportunities that come your way.
- It generates new ideas and unlocks success for each member of the group.
- The Master Mind is your very own board of directors, advising you, challenging you, and keeping you focused and accountable.
- An effective Master Mind group is made up of people with varying opinions and points of view.
- Your Master Mind should have a set of rules and guidelines that all the members agree to and dedicate themselves to.
- Dishonesty, negativity, selfishness, and being judgmental of the other members can derail your Master Mind right from the start.
- Practicing the Master Mind concept and dedicating yourself to it can exponentially increase your chances of success, fulfillment, and happiness in all areas of your life.

Worksheet #4

List the people in your life whom you feel a particularly strong connection to (family, friends, colleagues, etc.).

List the people in your life whom you feel you can completely trust.

List those people who seem to always have a different opinion than yours, but whom you respect.

If you could pick five people from history to be in your Master Mind group, who would they be and why?

What types of connections (communal, personal, professional, etc.) would be most beneficial to you in capturing your dreams?

What type of meeting format would you prefer for your Master Mind group? What would the rules be?

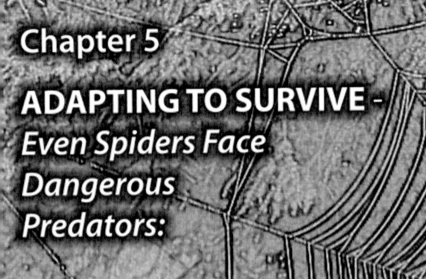

Chapter 5

ADAPTING TO SURVIVE -
*Even Spiders Face
Dangerous
Predators:*

OVERCOMING
ADVERSITY

*W*hen all kinds of trials and temptations crowd into your lives, my brothers, don't resent them as intruders, but welcome them as friends! Realize that they come to test your faith and to produce in you the quality of endurance.
—James 1:2–4

When we think of spiders, we normally think of them as predators. After all, they're the ones with the webs and the fangs. But spiders have their fair share of predators and other dangers, too.

Take the wasp, for example, one of the spider's most formidable enemies. When a female wasp locates a spider, she stings it and paralyzes it, but only temporarily. Then she lays an egg on her helpless prey. You can probably guess what happens next. Eventually the paralysis wears off, and the spider can move around again. But when the wasp egg hatches, the emerging larva begins to feed on the spider, sucking the fluid from its body. Then, when the larva is ready to enter its cocoon phase, it injects the spider with a chemical that makes the spider spin a type of tent, rather than a web. Finally, the larva kills the spider, eats it, and builds its cocoon inside the tentlike shelter, which was provided so kindly by the spider itself.

Talk about a gruesome ending.

And wasps aren't the spider's only predators. Birds, bats, frogs, toads, lizards, some types of fish, and praying mantises all have a taste for our eight-legged friends. Some spiders even prey on their own kind. And of course, human beings present a danger to spiders when we encroach on their natural habitats and when we kill them out of fear. In fact, of all the billions of spiders that are born every day on Earth, more than 99 percent of them die before reaching adulthood.

Over the millennia, spiders have been able to overcome many of these dangers through evolution and ingenuity. They have adjusted to different climates and atmospheric oxygen levels, and they have adapted to catch different types of prey and evade different types of predators.

Take the Namibian wheel spider, for example, which lives among the dunes of the Namib Desert in southern Africa. Whenever it is threatened by a wasp or other predator, the wheel spider folds in the outer ends of its legs and, flipping on its side, hurtles and bounces down the sandy slopes to safety.

When it comes to the obstacles in the way of your success and happiness, you need to take the same approach. No, you don't have to learn how to turn cartwheels. But you do need to be able to evolve and grow on a personal level, so that you can adapt to life's ever-changing circumstances and open yourself to the opportunities that are out there waiting to be caught.

Just like the spider, you too have many dangers—obstacles, setbacks, failures—that can prevent you from achieving your goals. Adversity is something that we all face from time to time. Spiders have adapted over time to deal with many of the dangers they face on a daily basis. You must do the same. As Napoleon Hill said, "Success is very largely a matter of adjusting one's self to the ever-varying and changing environments of life, in a spirit of harmony and poise." If you want to be successful in any endeavor and find the fulfillment you desire, you have to be able to deal with, overcome, and learn from adversity.

Dealing with Fear

The only thing we have to fear is fear itself.
—Franklin Delano Roosevelt

When FDR spoke these words, he was talking, of course, about fear of the enemy during World War II. If we could just find a way to get past our fears and focus on the objective, nothing could stand between us and absolute victory. And he was right.

The same can apply to your life. When you recognize the fears that paralyze you, those that hold you back from pursuing your passion and realizing your true purpose, you can then work to overcome these fears.

Take Greg, for example. For as long as he could remember, Greg wanted to be an entrepreneur. He dreamed of stepping completely out on his own and creating an organization that would not only support his life but create opportunities for others as well. There was only one thing holding him back: fear. Like many of us, Greg had found comfort and security in the world of corporate America. He was fearful of taking that risk and stepping headfirst into the swirl of instability that is entrepreneurship. He had fallen victim to the allure of financial security, the comforts of consistency, and the spoils of traveling a well-worn path. And for a wavering soul that is unconsciously following a predetermined script, playing it safe can provide a feeling of security and shelter.

Greg was following a far-too-familiar script that has been written, reviewed, and accepted by society: (1) Get a good education. (2) Pursue a career in a suitable profession. (3) Work hard at it. When you follow this formula, the rewards can be intoxicating—a hefty salary, stocks and bonuses, three-week vacations, a healthy pension for retirement, and so on.

But for Greg and many of us, this tale of happiness turns out to be nothing more than an illusion. Greg's financial security kept him seduced with all the trappings of success and influence, but he still lacked inner peace. He had a deep yearning to realize something greater than the so-called success he had come to know.

It wasn't easy for Greg to break free of the "American Dream" and wake up to his own incarnation of reality. His rational side, which was driven by fear, told him, "You've been here for over fifteen years now. Let's stay in the warm confides of corporate America, with its consistent professional progression, realizable cash flow, order, prestige, and influence." It was a convincing argument and one that stood in the way of Greg's dream to become an entrepreneur. The *reasonable* thing for him to do was to stay in his current position and continue to build his career. But as George Bernard Shaw says in his *Maxims for Revolutionists,* "The reasonable man adapts himself to the world: the unreasonable one persists in trying to adapt the world to himself. Therefore all progress depends on the unreasonable man." If he ever wanted to start his own company, Greg understood that he had to address his fears head-on and defeat them. He had to lose himself in order to find himself.

One of Greg's mentors and dear friends, Yvette Hayter-Adams, once presented him with an encased message: "Surround yourself with people who believe in your dreams." For Greg's dream to be realized, he knew it needed to be built on a sound foundation and supported by reliable resources. And that's exactly what he found when he began to build a strong core of individuals whom he could trust and depend on to keep him accountable—his Master Mind.

As a group we spent countless hours with Greg discussing the importance of living according to your God-given assignment, of living a purpose-driven life. These discussions were like workshops for the soul, and each was grounded in love, support, and brutal yet powerful honesty. It was through these conversations that Greg was able to recognize that fear was his strongest foe and the one thing that was preventing him from realizing his dream. Today he is the owner and partner of TriZen LLC, a business-consulting, leadership, and enterprise-development company, which designs the curriculum and facilitates the Urban Leadership Forum for the Urban League of Philadelphia. Through this company, Greg and his business partner, Tomeka Lee, identify and mentor emerging leaders from the region's premiere organizations.

Greg had the vision, and through the collective intelligence of the group, he was able to exorcise his fear and pursue that vision with energy, passion, and confidence.

Tangled Webs

Oh, what a tangled web we weave
When first we practise to deceive!
—Sir Walter Scott, *Marmion*

These poetic lines are just as true today as they were when Scott first penned them in 1808. When we're dishonest, especially with ourselves, no good can come from it. If you're not true to yourself—your unique personality, passions, and purpose—you'll get caught within a tangled web of lies and never be able to achieve what you want in this lifetime.

Say for example that you love music. In fact, you're a talented musician yourself, and nothing brings you more joy than when you're composing on your instrument. However, in order to pay the bills, you work in a job that provides no creative outlet, no way of expressing yourself like you do when you're playing music. Your job may provide the money you need to pay the mortgage and put food on the table, but is it allowing you to follow your passion? Is it helping you live according to God's assignment for your life—the only life you will ever have?

So do you do what you love and risk financial ruin, or do you play it safe and take the steady job that pays the bills? It's an all-too-common conundrum, one that's difficult if not impossible to answer on your own.

The summer before he entered college, Aki got an internship with AT&T through the INROADS program. At first it seemed like a good fit. He'd always had a passion for working with different kinds of people, and he was a fairly good leader. So he thought he could take those skills and excel in managing people in this position. It meant that he would have to ignore his love of the arts, but that was what his family told him to do. "You don't want to be a starving artist, do you?" So instead of honing his raw talents as a visual artist, actor, and writer, Aki decided to sharpen his business skills and majored in business management upon matriculating to the University of Pittsburgh.

During that first summer, Aki worked as an international telephone operator, connecting people to places like Russia and Cuba. It was tough at first because the other kids in the program teased him mercilessly. They were all working in true corporate settings and doing, at the very least, administrative work that would truly build their résumés and their skill sets, and here was Aki, working as a lowly operator. Or at least that's how they saw it.

After two whole summers of answering phone lines and plugging cords into a lighted phone board like the ones we've all seen in movies from the 1950s, Aki was actually given the opportunity to manage a team of operators in his second summer with the company. The teasing from interns with other corporate sponsors in the program quickly turned to envy. He was now walking with his chest out and beaming with pride in his ability to show leadership so early in his career. However, as he was given more and more responsibility, Aki became frustrated. Here he was, just nineteen years old, managing an entire team of adult operators. It was just too much for someone who had never even had a job before. In hindsight it was a great opportunity. But at the time, Aki was dealing with backlash and sabotage from some of his coworkers, and it was making him miserable. So, overwhelmed and unhappy, one day Aki just walked away from the job. He told his boss that he just couldn't do this anymore and that he wouldn't be back tomorrow.

Now, if Aki had been mature enough to take this opportunity to figure out exactly who he was and why he felt this way, if he had done some honest self-assessment, or even if there had been someone there to coach him, who understood Aki and who he was purposed to be, maybe he could have used this moment for growth. Instead, a month later, he went right back to that same internship. Those who guided him back there—friends and family members—really had no idea of who Aki was or who he was created to be, or they simply didn't accept that version of him. Though they believed they were acting in his best interest, they didn't understand his God-given assignment. Worst of all, Aki himself didn't understand what opportunities were out there that would make him happy and that would allow him to support himself through his passions. Aki simply wasn't honest with himself, and he accepted the dreams that others had for his life instead of trusting that his own dreams and passions were instilled in him for a reason. As a result, he went right back into a situation that was wrong for him, and it made him miserable. It wasn't until he began to do some honest introspection, to listen to his personal board of directors—his Master Mind counterparts—and most importantly, to listen to what God had been trying to tell him, that Aki was able to discover his true path and purpose in this world.

With the help of the Master Mind, Aki realized that his passion for working with people was indeed an asset and part of the fabric of who he was created to be. In fact, his name means "my brother" in Arabic. Relationships are what drive him, and his creative talents have coupled with that drive in a way that he would not have imagined for himself if he were left to rely solely on his own introspection.

Aki is not only fulfilling his passion and purpose in the coauthoring of this very book; he also intends to craft a screenplay that sheds light on the dysfunctional relationships between many mothers and their sons, write a book about how many of the lessons people need to learn for marriage are illustrated clearly for them during the planning of their wedding, and create a curriculum for marriage counseling that illustrates how one should appropriately operate as the parent of a married adult. He now operates as a relationship consultant and coach, providing insight and advisement services that fuel and accelerate growth through greater self-awareness and purposeful relationship building for individuals, couples, groups, organizations, and corporations. Aki could not be happier with the work he is doing today.

If you're not completely honest with yourself, you too may get caught in a situation that's not right for you. But when you're true to yourself, when you listen to your heart and allow God's assignment for you to take hold, then you will find a level of happiness and contentment you never knew was possible. Only through a dedicated system of introspection, faith, trust, and accountability, along with some honest, authentic, carefully considered advice from your most trusted connections, can you truly begin to figure out what is best for you as you move along your life's path. It's the only way you find out who you really are, what you really want, and how to go about getting it.

You can deceive yourself only so long. Eventually you will become tangled in your own web of lies and mismatched connections. Be true to yourself and others, and you'll be on the road to realizing your true purpose.

Knowing When to Abandon Your Web

A well-constructed and well-maintained web can help you catch your dreams and take you to the next level. But sometimes, no matter how hard you work to build and maintain your web, things can go wrong. And when this happens, you just have to cut your losses and start again.

Consider the spider. Maybe it thinks it has found the perfect spot for its web. So it carefully spins the web, taking great care to make it strong, flexible, and impenetrable. Then you come through with a broom, and in a flash, all the spider's hard work is gone.

The same thing can happen to you. You can take every precaution to make sure that you only connect with the right kinds of people. You can do your due diligence maintaining your web and making sure that it remains strong and flexible. But sometimes, no matter what you do, your web ends up weak and ineffective. Maybe your connections weren't as strong as you thought they were. Maybe they didn't hold up their end of the bargain. Then again, maybe it just wasn't the right time or place.

So, do you just give up? Of course not. Again, think about the spider. When its web gets suddenly wiped out by a broom or some animal, or if it fails to catch anything of significance, the spider doesn't give up. It starts over from scratch and builds again. Maybe it rebuilds in the same spot, hoping that the timing is better. Then again, maybe it moves on to another location altogether, where it knows the web will have a better chance of thriving. Sometimes spiders even eat their webs and recycle them into new, stronger silk.

The same applies to you. If your web isn't working out, take a close look at it and try to identify its weaknesses. Maybe it just needs a tweak here or there. Maybe you have to make the difficult decision to eliminate one or two of your connections to make room for someone else. Sometimes you may even have to consider abandoning your web altogether and starting over from square one. It's not the ideal situation, but it may be necessary if things are too far gone to repair. Just remember to be patient and thoughtful in your decisions. You're only human. Unlike a spider, you can't build an effective web overnight, and rash decisions can turn out to hurt you in the end.

You need to view abandoning your web merely as shifting your understanding of your relationships. Undoubtedly, there will be people you need to remove from your life. There will be others, however, who still have quality "silk" but who just don't have the proper strength or placement to help you capture what you want. This is where you have to decide if those relationships need to be cut from your web altogether or simply maintained and strengthened.

If you do end up having to abandon everything and start over, just remember to focus on the core. Most of the time, when your web becomes ineffective, it's because your center, your core, is weak. If you focus on rebuilding with a strong core of individuals whom you trust and admire above all others, that strength will radiate outward as you continue to make other strong, authentic connections.

Relationships always need to be renegotiated, even between a parent and child or a husband and wife. As we grow, mature, and change, so must our relationships. How you renegotiate those relationships is analogous to what the spider does with its web. Have you outgrown someone? If so, maybe you need to remove that line from your web because it can no longer support you or capture anything of substance for you. Then again, maybe you can do some general maintenance on the relationship—that is, respin it—and simply realign its placement in your web.

Just remember that it's OK to question your relationships from time to time. The trick is to learn when it's best to cut ties altogether and when you just need to give it a little TLC.

Personal Adversity

Sometimes no matter how vigilant you are in making sure your web is strong and well-placed, it still fails to help you catch what you want out of life. When this happens, it may be because of internal barriers. Personal adversity can be more detrimental to your web's effectiveness than anything else you encounter along your life's path. We already touched on fear and how it can hold you back. But there are other things that can also keep you from getting where you want to go and from catching the opportunities that are out there for you.

Negativity—This is one of the most common barriers that we deal with on a day-to-day basis. We all know the excuses:

> *I've already tried that, and it didn't work.*
> *This would never work for me.*
> *I don't have enough time.*
> *It's too hard.*
> *I don't have that many friends.*
> *I'm an introvert.*
> *I'm not smart enough.*
> *I don't trust anyone but myself.*
> *My situation is different.*

We could probably think of a dozen or more excuses to add to this list. And you know what? None of them would be valid. These are all examples of how negativity can poison the mind and prevent you from getting where you want to be in life. Napoleon Hill said it best: "There are no limitations to the mind except those we acknowledge. Both poverty and riches are the offspring of thought." Simply put, if you allow negative thoughts to dominate your mind, those negative influences will eventually reproduce themselves in your outward, physical world and become a reality.

When you get right down to it, negativity is rooted in fear—fear of failure, fear of hard work, fear of the unknown, fear of coming out of our shell and trying something new. It's a defense mechanism, a way of protecting yourself from getting hurt. Make commitment to yourself and your family that you will not allow someone else's fears to be transferred to you.

It's OK if you have a tendency to be negative. Many of us do. It's *not* OK, however, if you recognize your negativity and then do nothing about it. When you choose to be positive and open your mind to new ways of thinking, you open up yourself to a whole new world of opportunity and reward. Does this mean you will always find success? No. But that's life. Not everything is certain. But if you don't try, if you don't push aside your negativity and open your heart and mind, you will never know what you're really capable of.

One of the places negativity can be most damaging, as we mentioned earlier, is within your Master Mind group. When you or one of your group's members come in with a negative mind-set, it can drain the energy and power from the group altogether, leaving it lifeless and ineffective. Luckily, one of the Master Mind's greatest assets is its ability to shine a light on negativity and help the guilty party recognize his or her negative tendencies. And when this issue is finally out in the open, it can effectively be eliminated for the benefit of the group.

Lack of focus—Think about it in terms of taking a picture. When the subject is out of focus, the picture comes out blurry. And when the picture is blurry, it loses its inspirational power as an image. After all, the beauty is in the details.

We're all busy nowadays, and we all have a million and one things to distract us from our goals and blur our focus. Cell phones, smartphones, Twitter, Facebook, YouTube, e-mail, instant messaging, high-definition TV, on-demand TV, iPads, iPods—the list goes on and on. When used in moderation, these tools can actually add value to our lives. Then again, when they monopolize our time, they can distract us from our true purpose. The trick is finding the right balance and determining how to best leverage your time in order to get where you want to go. It's all about self-control and understanding what's really important to you. If you want to spend all your time playing the latest game on Facebook or browsing the latest apps on your smartphone, more power to you. But until you learn to prioritize your time and *focus* on your passions, you'll never truly find fulfillment and happiness. Focus on your true purpose, and pursue it with energy and steadfast determination. A spider never takes a break when constructing its web. It will press on until the task is completed, and then it will rest and reenergize within the strong and properly centered core—the Master Mind.

Lack of accountability—How many times in your life have you made a commitment to do something and then failed? How many New Year's resolutions have you failed to keep? How many promises have you made to change, only to find yourself stuck in the same old rut again? Too many times to count? Join the club.

Pledging to do something is one thing; following through with it is another thing altogether. Most of the time, the difference between accomplishment and failure can be attributed to one thing: accountability. You can have the best intentions in the world to do something, but if you're not held accountable, there's no guarantee that you'll accomplish what you set out to do. You have to learn to be accountable to yourself, and you have to have a trusted circle of friends and colleagues that will hold you accountable as well. That way, when you say you're going to do something, you can't just back out when the going gets tough. Your true friends won't let you quit that easily.

Again, this is where the Master Mind comes in. Your Master Mind group keeps you accountable. It doesn't let you be dishonest with yourself. It makes sure that you follow through on your intentions. It makes sure you stay on a path of growth and understanding that will help you get where you want to be in the long run. Remember, the spider will receive the strongest and most sensitive cues that there is something caught in the web when it is centered at its core.

Lack of confidence—Some people are born with confidence. They exude it. Others live their lives tormented by self-doubt. When you lack confidence, it can have a crippling effect and prevent you from trying anything new and from doing the things you need in order to pursue your passion. No matter what others tell them, some people think they're just not smart enough, funny enough, pretty enough, or talented enough. These individuals have a built-in disadvantage. They have to dig their way out of a hole before they can even think of beginning their journey.

Confidence isn't always easy to come by. And it's something that can be difficult to find on your own. That's why it's important to connect with others who can help you recognize your unique strengths and abilities and help you see that you really do have distinctive value. Sometimes we get so comfortable with our self-image that we fail to see ourselves as we truly are. You have to be able to step outside of yourself and see the "you" that everyone else sees.

Failure—That's right, failure. This book and the Spider Web Philsophy are most certainly about success and how to find it, but we are not offering you a fool proof approach to life that will exempt or protect you from falling down and outright losing at some point along your journey. English statesman Sir Winston Churchill, one of the most often quoted men in history, actually defined success as "the ability to go from one failure to another with no loss of enthusiasm." Failure is a necessary step in the process. Don't let your natural apprehensions and the emotional sting of failure keep you from moving forward with boldness and passion.

When you lack the audacity to take calculated risk because of your fear of failure, then lean on your Master Mind and allow them to serve as the natural cheerleaders that they are. Remember, this team is fully invested in you. Your connection to it may not guarantee you a win in this moment, but it is there to insure that you fail forward and help you take the measured steps you need to prevail in the long run. Let them lend you their assurance when you lack self-assurance. Churchill also famously said that "Success is not final, failure is not fatal: it is the courage to continue that counts." Our ultimate success is not always an indicator that we have avoided failure. Success doesn't necessarily happen for us in spite of failure. Our success is often the result of our failures and how we have responded to them.

What type of personal adversity are you facing? What are your fears? Are you being true to yourself? Are you following your passions and pursuing your true purpose in life, or are you just drifting along aimlessly, hoping that things will change? You can't change your situation and overcome the obstacles that are standing in your way without finding the answers to these questions. And you can't be sure you're being totally honest with yourself unless you have others whom you can trust to back up your evaluation, help put you on the right path, and keep you accountable in the process.

Napoleon Hill said, "Many successful people have found opportunities in failure and adversity that they could not recognize in more favorable circumstances." Everyone faces adversity in life. Each of us has a different journey and faces different obstacles, setbacks, and failures. What's important is how you react and adapt to these things and how you use them to your advantage.

Chapter 5 Takeaways
So let's review:

- We all face adversity and find obstacles standing in the way of our success and happiness. Until we address and overcome this adversity, we will never find contentment in life.
- Fear is a powerful obstacle that can prevent us from pursuing our passions and finding our true purpose in life. We cannot grow as individuals until we recognize our fears and learn to deal with them.
- You must be completely honest with yourself about your true passions and desires.
- It's OK to question your relationships from time to time. The trick is to learn when you just need to devote a little time to saving and strengthening the relationship and when it's best to cut ties altogether.
- If you want to be successful in any endeavor, you must have a trusted group of people to help keep you accountable and on track.
- Your success is not predicated on the avoidance of failure, but it is determined by how you manage failure.
- Whether adversity comes from external sources or from within, you have to learn how to adapt to it, deal with it, and learn from it.

Worksheet #5

What fears hold you back from accomplishing your goals and dreams?

What steps can you take to overcome your fears?

Have you ever had to abandon a relationship, either personal or professional? How did it affect you?

Do you have relationships in your life right now that simply need to be renegotiated or realigned?

Write about a time when you weren't truthful with yourself and how it affected you negatively.

Which people in your current networks can you trust to hold you accountable and on track?

Write about a your toughest loss or your greatest failure. How did it impact you? In general, what did you learn from it? What did it teach you about yourself? Have you or will you over come it and, if so, how?

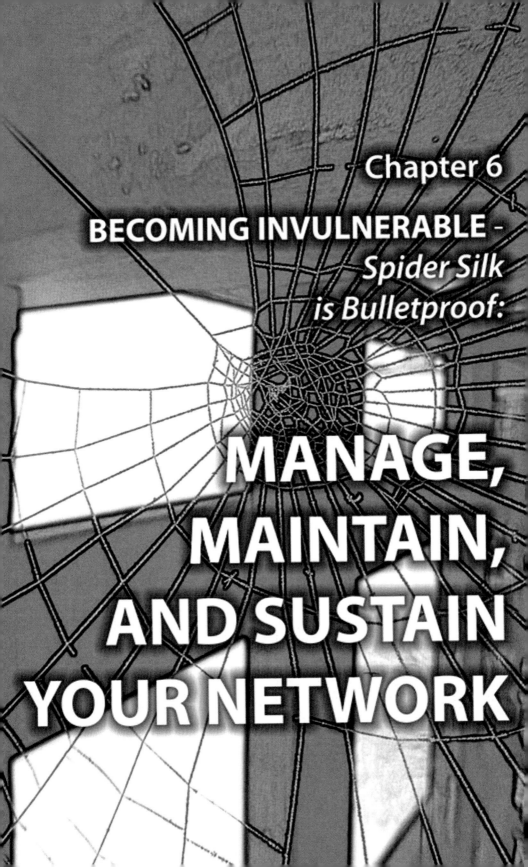

Chapter 6

BECOMING INVULNERABLE – *Spider Silk is Bulletproof:*

MANAGE, MAINTAIN, AND SUSTAIN YOUR NETWORK

Back in 1881 at Tombstone, Arizona, a physician named Emery Goodfellow was attending to a man who'd been killed in a gun battle. Goodfellow pulled a silk handkerchief from the victim's breast pocket, and inside he found the two bullets that had struck the man in the chest. The bullets themselves never penetrated the man's body—they had been stopped cold by the silk handkerchief! It was the impact of the projectiles that proved fatal.

Silk, specifically spider silk, is pound-for-pound one of the strongest materials known to man. Its tensile strength is greater than that of high-grade steel. The silk of Darwin's bark spider is said to be more than ten times stronger than Kevlar, the synthetic fiber used in bulletproof vests. For years scientists have been trying to recreate spider silk in the lab, and they're getting closer every day. It's quite possible that silks could one day be used to create body armor that's more lightweight and flexible than what we have today. And since silks do not elicit an immune response, they may also have valuable biomedical applications, such as in artificial tendons.

When it comes to building your web, you want it to be made with the strongest "silk" possible. A weak web is of no use to you. If you can't depend on your web's connections, you can't expect it to help you catch the kinds of opportunities you're looking for. Of course, you also want your web to be flexible, just like a spider's web, so that it can grow with you and adapt to the ever-changing circumstances of your life.

You want your web to be invulnerable and unstoppable. You want it to be bulletproof.

Manage. Maintain. Sustain.

So how do you do this? First, you have to make sure that your web is made up of authentic relationships. Remember, a chain is only as strong as its weakest link. The same is true of your web. You have to make sure that each of your connections is someone you can trust and depend on. You have to be certain that you can count on them to provide honest feedback, that they will be accountable, and that they possess some unique wisdom or talent that can help you get where you want to be.

But that's not all. Just as the human body needs regular care and exercise, unless you work to maintain your web and keep it in shape, it will become weak and of no use to you.

Consider the cobweb. Lifeless and empty, hanging from basement rafters and in the corner of the garage—cobwebs are the ruins of spider webs past. By definition, a cobweb is an abandoned web. As a trap for insects, it is no longer effective or useful. It has lost its true purpose. Sure, it can get plenty of things to stick to it—dust, leaves, the tiniest insects with no nutritional value—but the quality of the silk has long since eroded with time. It now lacks the strength, elasticity, and stickiness of a well-maintained web. You might even say it is no longer authentic.

When you fail to keep your web strong and in good working order, it too can become like a cobweb—ineffective, useless, without purpose. If you want to make your web bulletproof, you have to manage, maintain, and sustain it. Just as the spider regularly eats, recycles, and respins its web, you too have to continually analyze your web to make sure that your connections are strong, that you're consistently checking in with them to see how you can best serve them, and that they're integral to you catching your aspirations and achieving your God-given purpose.

When you're doing this type of web maintenance, try to identify your relationships that are completely one-sided and take more than they give. These types of connections can sap your web's strength, and they're not doing anything to serve you. As we mentioned earlier, you may need to cut these connections from your web altogether. Communication is key in this process. You can't know whether you need to eliminate a relationship or simply renegotiate it without clear communication between both parties. You also have to have the right mixture of purposeful communication and a more casual, touching-base style of communication.

Of course, this mixture is different for just about everybody. For example, Grandma likes it when you pop in for a visit or give her a call once in a while without any prior notice. On the other hand, your supervisor hates surprises and instead requires a scheduled time and agenda for every meeting or call. Each person in your life has his or her own preferred way of communicating and staying in touch. Sometimes these lines can get blurred in relationships that require a little bit of each style. In order to keep them strong and of value to you, take the time to analyze your relationships carefully and decide how much time you need to devote to each.

Developing and maintaining meaningful, authentic relationships isn't something that can be done overnight. It takes time and patience. Sometimes you just click with someone and have a special chemistry that immediately bonds the two of you. This is the exception, however, rather than the norm. Most authentic relationships take months or even years to cultivate, and you're never really sure when your dedication to that person will come back to benefit you in your particular path in life. But as long as you are diligent and steadfast, eventually you'll reap the rewards of your efforts.

When you're maintaining your web, there are things that you can do along the way to ensure that your connections keep you in the front of their minds and that they think of you in a positive light. Although these things may seem inconsequential or time-consuming, they are absolutely vital in sustaining a strong, dependable, effective web:

Send small tokens of appreciation—This is a great way to stay in someone's mind, which is extremely important when it comes to catching an opportunity. It can be something as little as a sending a greeting card, handwriting a personal note, or maybe even giving the person a ten-dollar gift card to his or her favorite café. Remember, it's the thought that counts. Take the time to brighten someone's day, and it will keep you in the front of that person's mind.

Show them that you care—People love to know that others truly care about them. Make a point to reach out to your connections regularly and show a sincere interest in their well-being. Send a quick e-mail, or even better, draft a brief letter asking how things are going and if there's anything you can do for them. When you show people that you care, it tells them that they're important to you, and in turn, it helps strengthen the bonds of your relationship.

Spend time honoring the connection—E-mails and notes are great ways to stay in touch with your connections. But if you really want to build strong, lasting, authentic relationships, if you really want to understand others' passions and aspirations and the challenges that they're facing, you have to schedule some regular face-to-face time with them. Make maintaining your relationships a priority. Schedule regular meetings with your connections, and stick to them. If you do, your relationships will be stronger and more valuable to you in the long run.

Of course, these are just a few of the ways you can begin to make your web bulletproof. Each situation is different. It's up to you to recognize what you have to offer that can help other people catch their objectives and achieve their goals. Just remember to always put the needs of others first and do whatever you can to be a valuable, dependable, authentic connection.

Manage. Maintain. Sustain. This is the mantra for a strong, effective, bulletproof web.

Buckshot versus Focused Fire

Say, for example, you go to a professional conference somewhere and, over the course of the weekend, you collect one hundred business cards. That's great, as long as you plan to reach out and connect with those people within the next week to start to build relationships with them. But let's be honest, when you meet people at a conference, it's difficult even to remember what each person looked like, let alone what made you want to build relationships with them.

But what if you went to that same conference, and instead of collecting as many business cards as you could, you focused on connecting with just two or three people who you felt particularly drawn to? What if you spent your time really listening to and getting to know those individuals and helping them understand your own goals and passions as well? More than likely you'd reap greater rewards from making a few solid, meaningful connections than making one hundred or more casual ones. When it comes to building an impenetrable, bulletproof web, it's quality, not quantity, that counts.

Think about it in terms of sunlight. On its own it can generate power, but you need to collect a lot of it, which can take a lot of time and space. But when sunlight is focused and concentrated on a single point, as through a magnifying glass, its power is immediately intensified, and it can even spark a flame. As George Fraser says: "Power is most effective concentrated. You can take a 55-gal. drum of water, spill it over, it will disperse, find its own level, and eventually evaporate. You can take that same 55-gal. drum of water, put it under pressure, put a lid on it, put a hose in it, put a nozzle on the end of that hose, and it can cut concrete."

There is greater power in focus. Focus on building strong, reliable, authentic relationships, and if you do, your web will have great power and yield greater results. Just remember, even two or three solid connections will become useless and ineffective in time unless you continually strive to grow and strengthen them.

Manage. Maintain. Sustain.

Right-Sizing Your Web

When it comes to your web, size matters. But how big should it be? Nowadays, with the exponential growth of social networking, it seems like it's all about the numbers:

> *I have over seven hundred Facebook friends.*
> *My Twitter account has over five hundred followers.*
> *I have more than one thousand connections on LinkedIn!*

That's great, but what kind of results are these numbers yielding? If your Twitter following helps you get noticed by someone who ends up hiring you based on your tweets, more power to you. If your Facebook account helps you find a kindred spirit who ends up being your soul mate, that's wonderful, too. Unfortunately, you can't depend on this type of serendipity.

If you want to guarantee that your web will help you catch your dreams, you don't have to try to make as many connections as possible. Rather, you have to make sure that it's right-sized for you. It has to fit your unique personality and your preferred way of doing things. You could have a thousand "friends" or followers, but if they're not working for you, if they're not getting you where you want to be, what good are they? On the other hand, you may only have fifteen connections, but if they're all truly authentic and provide you with advice and feedback that helps you grow as a person and move in the direction of your true purpose, isn't that all you really need?

Your ability to trust, your willingness to socialize, and your capacity for intimacy all help to determine the size of your web. Aki, for example, is a social butterfly. We actually call him "The Mayor" because it seems like everywhere we go, Aki always knows everybody in the room. Through his creative initiatives—acting, emceeing, public speaking—he has been able to make a lot of valuable connections that have paid dividends in his career. In contrast to Aki's expansive web, Wesley's is smaller in scope. Even though everyone loves to be around him, his laser focus and intense discipline do not lend themselves to creating the large number of connections that Aki makes through his creativity.

Aki's and Wesley's individual webs may differ in size, but that's OK. They are tailored to their personalities and their preferred methods of connecting with others. Most important, each has many strong, authentic connections. Furthermore, through their common web, Wes gets the benefit of Aki's expansive network, and Aki gets the benefit of Wes's laser focus. So it's a win-win for both.

The key here, again, is to concentrate on the quality of your relationships rather than the number. Quality versus quantity. Eventually you may end up building a large web with hundreds of connections, such as Aki's, and if that's what you need in order to catch your dreams, there's nothing wrong with that. But when you're first starting to build your web, focus more on making sure your relationships are strong. The rest will come with time.

Growing and Strengthening Your Web

Each one of us has one comprehensive web that's made up of all of our connections and relationships. However, as we mentioned in the introduction, this larger web is made up of a lot of smaller webs. Your family is a web. Your coworkers make up another web. Your friends, your church members, the other people in your book club, and so on—these too are webs. You should, however, have one solid core web that serves as your foundation, one that you depend on above all others.

Once your core is strong and you start building outward on your web, you'll want to consider leveraging parts or all of your existing webs. Maybe you have a coworker whom you feel particularly close to, whom you can trust, and whom you feel may have something to offer in helping you get where you want to be. Maybe you have another group of secondary friends outside of your core group of friends that can bring some value. In addition, there may be certain people in your church congregation whom you admire and trust and with whom you feel a special connection.

If you want to make your web bulletproof, you need to consider including connections from all of your life's webs. If you're going to include people from your other webs, just be sure to only consider those individuals who you are certain will strengthen and bring something of value. Remember, you always want to think about adding *authentic* relationships. Each person in your web must bring something to the table. Each must be someone whom you can trust and who has skills and knowledge that can help take you where you want to go. Furthermore, each must be someone to whom you are able to offer something as well. After all, the Spider Web Philosophy is as much about giving as about taking. As Martin Luther King Jr. once said, "Life's most persistent and urgent question is, 'What are you doing for others?'"

In your everyday life, you should always be on the lookout for valuable new connections. You always have to have your feelers out there and be looking and listening for individuals who can strengthen and grow your web. The four of us are always meeting new people, and when we do, we always consider whether or not these individuals would be good additions to our webs. You should be doing the same thing in your daily interactions. Pay attention to the people you meet. Ask about what they do, and really listen to them. Discover what new ideas they may have offer. Find out what they're looking for in life and how you may be able to help them catch it.

The world is getting smaller every day. Now, more than ever, we have access to more people and whatever knowledge and talents they may possess. So keep your eyes open and your ears peeled—you never know who is going to cross your life's path today. Sometimes God leads us to others who he knows can help us find our way in life. You never know when you're going to meet someone that will change your life for the better—someone that will help make your web bulletproof.

Chapter 6 Takeaways

So let's review:

- Manage, maintain, and sustain your web. Analyze your relationships regularly, and understand how much time you need to devote to each in order to keep them strong and thriving.
- Do little things for others to ensure that they keep you in the front of their minds and that they think of you in a positive light.
- You don't have to have thousands of connections to get you where you want to go. You just have to have right kinds of connections with people who understand who you are and what you're trying to accomplish. Right-size your web specifically for you.
- There is greater power in focus. Focus on building strong, reliable, authentic relationships, and your web will yield greater results.
- Leverage your other webs to grow and strengthen your network. Choose only those individuals you know you can depend on to keep you moving forward toward your goal.
- Focus on quality, not quantity.
- Do unto others as you would have them do to you. It's the Golden Rule of life and of the Spider Web Philosophy.
- Always be on the lookout for new, authentic connections.

Worksheet #6

Write about a time when you had to cut someone out of your life. How did it benefit you?

Have you ever had to reconnect with someone? What was the hardest part of the process?

Identify a few of your closest relationships and write about how they differ in the type and frequency of communication they require.

What other webs do you have that you can leverage or farm from in order to catch your desired goal?

Write about a group or organization you had to abandon and what you learned from the experience.

Write about a group or organization that you chose to stick with and that ended up helping you grow.

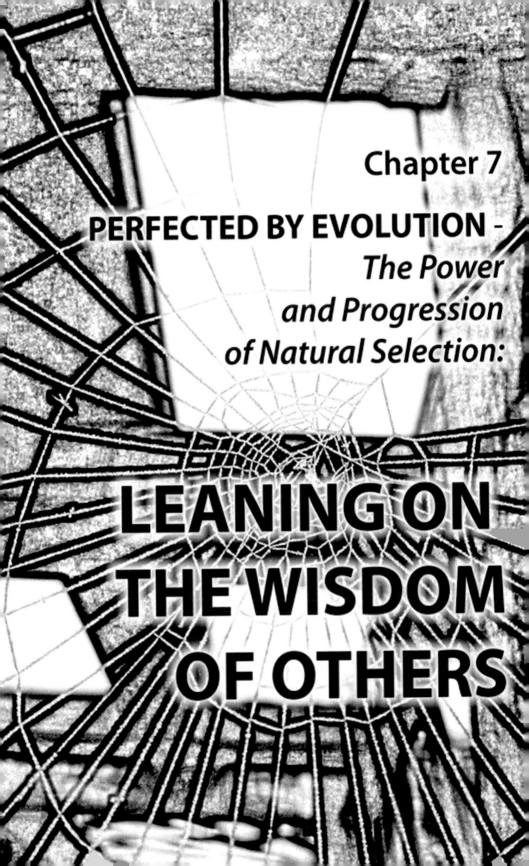

Chapter 7

PERFECTED BY EVOLUTION -
The Power
and Progression
of Natural Selection:

LEANING ON
THE WISDOM
OF OTHERS

The spider is the epitome of efficiency. It doesn't waste time or energy chasing after its prey. Instead it selects a spot where its prey is mostly likely to come on its own, and then it sets up camp, building a strong, inescapable trap to catch whatever comes along.

Spiders have evolved over millions of years, building on lessons learned from those that came before them. They learned to adapt to various environments. They figured out what worked and what didn't. Gradually, they developed into the lethal killers they are today.

In order for you to get where you want to be in life, you can't do it alone. No matter how smart you are or how thorough you are or how hard you work to achieve your goals, you still have to learn from others. You have to be willing to tap the wisdom they have gained through their own experiences and then apply it to your own life in a way that will advance you toward your goals and purpose. If don't learn from the mistakes of others, you are doomed to repeat them yourself. Why waste all that time and energy when others have already paved the way for you?

In *Leadership Gold*, John C. Maxwell says, "The willingness to seek and accept advice is a great indicator of accountability. If you seek it early—before you take action—you will be less likely to get off track. Most wrong actions come about because people are not being held accountable early enough."

Whatever you're going through, there's someone else out there who's already been through it and learned from it. The wisdom you're looking for is out there. You just have to know where to look.

Mentoring

As a youngster, Ellen Langas knew she had the potential for greatness, but she had little influence from her family to develop personal or professional goals. However, when she was a freshman in college, there was one professor who encouraged her to work hard, set goals, and follow her dreams. He served as a mentor to Ellen and encouraged her to get involved in the SIFE (Students in Free Enterprise) program. Eventually, she headed up her school's team and ended up leading the team to its first-ever SIFE USA National Championship. She went on to graduate summa cum laude and eventually earned her MBA.

Today Ellen is the president and founder of NouSoma Communications Inc. (nousoma.com), a public relations and marketing company. Prior to that she was an officer and popular on-air personality for QVC Inc. In 1994 she was named Mrs. Pennsylvania, and four years later she was named one of the state's best fifty women in business.

Ask Ellen today, and she'll tell you that much if not all of her professional success can be traced back to that one professor, that mentor, who encouraged her to set goals and to try things that were out of her comfort zone. Most important of all, he was there to keep her accountable.

"The best mentors can help you identify your strengths and weaknesses and show you how to focus on your strengths, providing honest, positive, and detailed feedback," she says. "The experience was life-changing. I was so moved by the support and coaching that this professor extended to me, that I was determined to pay it forward."

Ellen is also the author of the Girls Know How® series (girlsknowhow. com), which encourages young girls to "explore careers and follow their dreams." "Mentoring is all about helping another grow," says Ellen. "You should always focus on what you can give rather than what you can get from the relationship."

The passion and purpose Ellen developed through the mentoring relationship she had with her professor unfolded over the years. Eventually she became an education advocate. "I've embarked on many efforts to encourage young people to explore the careers of their dreams and acquire the skills necessary to achieve them."

Mentoring is an essential part of the Spider Web Philosophy—mentoring others and having mentors yourself. Both are important in your personal and professional growth, and both are important steps in helping you get where you want to be.

For all of us, our Master Mind group is a mentor in itself. Outside of that, we each have many people we consider mentors, some whom we know personally and some whom we'll never meet. Individuals like Napoleon Hill, for example. We also have our personal mentors—our families and friends—as well as our professional mentors, those whom we look up to for the value-driven way in which they operate. Over the years we've found people who've advised and counseled us on various projects and assignments, and we still reconnect with them regularly.

Of course, we all also serve as mentors to others, because we believe that servant leadership is an important element in creating authentic connections. We should be accountable to others and help them in their particular journeys in life.

Greg, for example, in addition to working with Big Brothers Big Sisters, has had the opportunity to form coaching relationships with many of Philadelphia's emerging leaders through the Urban Leadership Forum. Through the program, he gets to discuss with these individuals everything from self-branding and community to organization, legacy, and more.

Daniel Darling (danieldarling.com), senior pastor of Gages Lake Bible Church in the northwest suburbs of Chicago and author of *Teen People of the Bible, Crash Course,* and *iFaith,* understands the value of the mentor/mentee relationship. In a guest post on Michael Hyatt's blog, michaelhyatt.com, Pastor Darling says that a mentor's value "cannot be overestimated... A mentor is someone who is a few laps ahead of you in an area of life where you wish to find success. More than formal training, more than a book or a seminar, a good mentor brings his or her personal experience to bear on your life in a way that may shape it forever."

Darling also advises people on how to find a mentor. "Don't start with Seth Godin or Max Lucado," he says. "Instead, look for someone a few levels ahead of you in your chosen field. Someone accessible to you."

He also suggests attending community events or gatherings, sparking up conversations with people, and letting "natural human interaction be your guide." Then, after you've planted the seeds of a relationship, follow up with the person and request to meet with him or her again sometime. It can be as simple as asking the person if you can buy him or her a cup of coffee. "Mentoring relationships are valuable...and they aren't complicated," says Darling. "They are simply friendships which have the potential to help shape your future."

From high school through the early years of his career, George Burrell Jr. was influenced by men and women who took a serious interest in his well-being. These mentors taught him that despite the accomplishments of history's great men and women, our goals, values, and accomplishments are much more influenced by the people who play a direct role in our lives, people like teachers and parents. And it's people like them who showed him the value of mentoring.

Burrell is a senior executive vice president and COO of Universal Companies. Previously, he was a partner in Kleinbard Bell & Brecker LLPand a member of the firm's government-relations practice, where he advised business clients on strategic planning and government relations. From 1980 to 1984, he served as deputy mayor of Philadelphia to Mayor William Green and was an at-large member of the Philadelphia City Council. Today he is a member of the Pennsylvania Convention and Visitors Bureau's board of directors, the Center City District, and the Community College Foundation. He is also a former trustee of the University of Pennsylvania and a past chairman of the Urban League of Philadelphia and has served on the boards of the National Bar Association, the African American Museum, the Pennsylvania Convention Center, the Kimmel Center for the Regional Performing Arts, and the National Adoption Center. And before all that, in 1969, he was a starting defensive back for the Denver Broncos.

Burrell has benefitted from the various mentor/mentee relationships he's formed over the years. In his second year of law school, a man by the name of Ragan Henry hired Burrell as an associate in his firm. "He helped make me a good lawyer and taught me how to develop a client base," he says.

Another mentor was former congressman William H. Gray. "Bill Gray was not only instrumental to my political career but was also my pastor and is one of my closest friends. Those relationships exposed me to opportunities and experiences I may not have had as early in my career."

And it was these experiences, these close relationships, that taught Burrell the value of mentoring.

In 1985, with the help of his partner at Kleinbard, former congressman Gray, David Hyman, and other Jewish and African American community leaders, Burrell cofounded Operation Understanding, a program that sends African American and Jewish high-school juniors to Israel and Africa annually. Over the years he has mentored many of the young people who have come through the program and remains integral in their lives today.

As the first president of the Black Alumni Society at Penn, Burrell has been a mentor to many students over the years with whom he still interacts to this day. "I have tried to make myself available to those who reach out and provide them with the best advice I can," he says. "Having been blessed to have a variety of successes and public failures in my career, I often get approached by young people who tell me my career and their following of it has influenced them positively. My experiences with young people and the impact I have on their lives is important to me."

Once you determine where your passion lies and where you want it to take you, don't try to get there on your own. Find others who have already climbed that mountain, mine their wisdom, and apply it to your own unique situation. And when you get to the top of your mountain, don't forget to do what you can to pull others up as well.

Coaching

A good mentor can help you discover your true talents and then set you on the path to make the most of your God-given gifts. But just because you've found a certain level of success in your career and fulfillment in your life, it doesn't mean that you shouldn't still seek out the counsel of others—those who may be able to see you from an unbiased point of view and give you the kind of advice and guidance you need to take yourself to the next level.

Think about it. Even the most successful athletes have coaches to help them improve on their mechanics and, in turn, their overall game. And the same goes for you. It is absolutely critical in your journey that you seek out objective, honest help and support. After all, you can't always see the big picture when you are in the frame.

The International Coach Federation (coachfederation.org), the global governing body for the coaching industry, defines coaching as "partnering with clients in a thought-provoking and creative process that inspires them to maximize their personal and professional potential."

Remind you of anything? It's almost like a one-to-one Master Mind group. Just ask professional coach Jill Mazza.

"The coaching space is where clarity is mined, insights are generated and action plans are created," she says. "And insight without action is nothing but watered-down hope."

Mazza is the owner of Pittsburgh-based Mazza Coaching (mazzacoaching.com). She says that the essence of mentoring and coaching is the relationship between two people. "Coaching is a process that can help us to more clearly see the meaning behind our connections," she says. "It's about becoming more consciously aware of who we are and how we choose to show up in life, in order to make smarter decisions in alignment with our true intentions and core values."

Although mentoring and coaching have a lot of similarities, Mazza says there is a distinct difference between the two. "Mentoring often occurs in educational and professional settings where the mentor has more experience and tenure within an industry, organization or specific roles/tasks than the mentee. The phrase 'to take someone under our wing' comes to mind with mentoring. A professional coach does not mentor or 'take someone under their wing', so to speak. A professional coach is a trusted, strategic partner who is on equal footing with the client. The client is the expert in his or her life; the coach is expert in coaching and holds the client's agenda while helping the client to maximize personal and professional potential around stated goals."

Coaching is something that Mazza has felt drawn to since a young age. "When I was a little girl I drew a picture of several rings connected to each other. When my mother asked me to explain the drawing, I told her that each ring represented a life, and that every life is connected to another life at a certain point, exactly when it is supposed to for a certain reason. In adulthood, I have always referred to the 'Table of My Inner Circle'—the people whom I hold close and from whom I value insights. The Spider Web Philosophy and the concept of a personal Board of Directors really resonate with me.

"I believe that coaching is one of my God-given purposes that allows me to help people to approach life with more conscious awareness and high-level energy."

Mazza, who obtained her professional-coaching certification from the Institute for Professional Excellence in Coaching (ipeccoaching.com) in 2009, began taking clients one month after becoming certified and has maintained a small, steady practice ever since. "Coaching has undoubtedly changed how I see myself and influences the energetic choices I make in life and at work. While I knew having a coaching certification would make me more valuable in my work as a corporate communications trainer, I also choose to pursue my coach training out of my own desire for continuous personal and professional development."

Mazza is interested in understanding how we can each become closer to our best selves every day. "Relationships in life and at work are mirrors to measure our progress." Life coaching is one of her specialties, although she's not a fan of the term itself. "I think the label 'Life Coach' is overused and nebulous. To say that a coach coaches a client on life is too broad. While making positive changes and achieving stated goals in one area of our lives often has cascading effects in other areas, effective coaching programs tend to focus on one or two specific areas of personal or professional life so that maximum results can be achieved through forced focus. This is where coaching niches come into play and how coaches differentiate themselves within the profession. My passions are people, relationships and how we communicate in them."

As a certified professional coach specializing in improving communication skills and emotional self-management, Mazza positions herself as a communication coach, helping clients communicate with increased control, clarity, and confidence on the job and in personal relationships. "My communication coaching niche continues to evolve as I gain more corporate training experience, cocreate more coaching partnerships with individual clients and move through my own life."

You've probably heard the old adage that good therapists have good therapists. Well, the same goes for coaches. Mazza has been meeting with her chosen professional coach on a weekly basis since she began her professional-coach training in 2008. "My coach has a permanent seat on my personal Board of Directors. We have a powerful bond and solid working relationship that help me to maintain objectivity and self-awareness when things are going well, and when they're not going so well."

Mazza believes that our lives, careers, and relationships are what we make of them. Coaching helps her see herself more clearly and plan how she wants to show up in life more strategically. "What my clients work on, I work on. When appropriate, I self-disclose what I am working on with my coach in my life, with my clients, to deepen our mutual scope of experience and awareness and ultimately enhance insights and key learning."

Unfortunately, today, many people don't see professional coaching as a serious endeavor. According to Mazza, the most common misconception about coaches is that there is no solid educational or professional foundation on which to base the profession and subsequent coaching services. "There are a lot of so-called coaches out there who aren't certified by programs recognized by the International Coach Federation. People promote themselves as coaching experts on everything from breathing to spirituality to finding life purpose and passion. It is no wonder that the general public is skeptical of certain coaches and the industry."

She says that, when you're looking for a coach, it is important to confirm that the person is professionally certified. "It is essential for the coach to have demonstrated personal and/or professional success and credentials in the areas in which they claim to specialize." She says it's best to have a phone or face-to-face consultation first to ensure that both parties understand the process and also to determine if there is a coaching match. "Look for coaches who demonstrate an understanding of your learning and communication styles and with whom you feel you can be deeply honest and fully present; who you think will push you beyond your comfort zones. The power of coaching lies in the synergy between client and coach. There has to be client/coach chemistry. Once an authentic connection is made, the coaching partnership can develop from a solid foundation of trust, honesty and accountability toward the achievement of the client's stated goals."

In general, Mazza says, people who benefit from coaching are interested in continuous personal and professional development, are willing to practice self-reflection and self-management, and are able to receive constructive feedback. "Coaching is about accountability," says Mazza. "Clients must consciously choose to be accountable to themselves and to the coaching partnership and process to maintain momentum toward stated goals. The client must choose to be accountable to take action toward the changes they say they want. He or she must be willing to take full personal responsibility for their thoughts, feelings, and actions. The coach holds the client accountable."

Determine your purpose, and then find a coach to help get you there.

Chapter 7 Takeaways
So let's review:

- You can't get where you want to be in life alone.
- Mentoring is an essential part of the Spider Web Philosophy—both mentoring others and having mentors yourself.

- Be accountable to others and help them in their particular journeys in life.
- Determine your purpose, and then find a coach to help get you there.
- Even the most successful athletes have coaches to help them improve on their mechanics and their overall game. The same goes for you.

Worksheet #7

Who in your life has served as a mentor to you?

What wisdom did you gain from this relationship(s)?

If you could choose anyone to mentor you, past or present, who would it be and why?

Have you ever mentored someone else, and if so, how were you able to change his or her life?

What did you learn from being a mentor?

Have you ever had a life coach, and if so, what did you find most valuable about the experience?

What particular area of your life would most benefit from a coaching relationship?

Chapter 8

ENSNARING YOUR DREAMS –
Packaging Your Catch for Future Consumption:

WRAPPING IT ALL UP

When a spider does everything right; when it carefully follows its instincts and builds its web according to the plan that's been honed and passed down through the ages; when it places its web in the perfect location and uses only the strongest of silk to anchor it in place; when it builds everything around a solid core; when it does all of these things, it fulfills its God-given assignment here on Earth. It realizes its true purpose.

The same goes for you and your web. When you build it through the principles we have laid out in this tested and proven philosophy, principles that have worked not only for us but for the successful individuals we highlighted in this book, you can expect to discover a level of happiness and fulfillment like never before.

The Spider Web Philosophy is something we developed over many years, through our many successes and failures. It is founded on the principles and lessons of people like Napoleon Hill, George Fraser, and others, who understand the power of connectivity. By tapping the knowledge of these wise and inspirational individuals and synthesizing their knowledge into a unified, practical, purposeful philosophy, we have created a system that has been invaluable in our own lives. And we know it can be just as life-changing for you.

The Spider Web Philosophy doesn't present anything new; it doesn't reveal some unknown truth. Rather, it is the opening of one's mind to something that already exists. It is a paradigm shift, enabling you to see things in an entirely new way. We're not claiming to have discovered some new way of thinking. Napoleon Hill did the grunt work back in the early 1900s. We just took what he discovered and built on that foundation, using George Fraser's metaphor of the spider web in order to develop a philosophy and a way of living that we know can help take you to the next level, wherever or whatever that may be for you.

Just remember, the Spider Web Philosophy is not a solution; it's a way of life. You have to live it every day and constantly work at it in order for it to produce your desired results. But as long as you dedicate yourself to its principles and stick with it over time, you'll create a far-reaching, bulletproof web capable of catching even the most elusive of dreams.

Wrapping It All Up

Let's review some of the main takeaways of the Spider Web Philosophy:

- It's not about what you know or who you know. It's about who knows you and what they think about you.
- When you cultivate strong, authentic relationships over time, you can then leverage those relationships to catch your dreams, goals, and ambitions.
- The Master Mind is your web's core. It's where you can rest, reenergize, and be ready to catch the opportunities that come your way; it is your personal board of directors, advising you, challenging you, and keeping you focused and accountable.
- You are unique; your web must be unique to you and what you want out of life.
- You have to strategically "place" your web—that is, you have to make the right connections based on what you are trying to catch.
- Fear is a powerful obstacle that can prevent you from pursuing your passions and finding your true purpose in life. You have to recognize your fears and deal with them.
- Whether adversity comes from external sources or from within, you have to learn how to adapt to it, deal with it, and learn from it.
- In order for your web to be bulletproof, you have to manage, maintain, and sustain it.
- No matter where you want to be in life, you can't get there alone.

It all comes back to the spider. The spider doesn't pursue its prey, expending valuable energy and increasing its chances of failure. It channels its energy into building a "bulletproof" web in an opportune location, where it knows its prey is most likely to come. Then it sits and waits, conserving energy and eventually reaping the benefits of its perfectly constructed trap.

As we've seen in this book, this doesn't just work for our eight-legged friends—it works for people, too. When you build strong, authentic connections, you no longer have to expend enormous amounts of time and energy chasing after dreams that you may never realize on your own. The perfect web will help you catch what you truly want from life.

Your dreams are waiting—go catch them!

About the Authors

The DAWG team (a play on the group's first-name initials and the slang terminology for friendship)

Dwight, Aki, Wesley, and Greg have been forging and cementing their friendships since their early high-school days. Dwight and Wesley Pullen are siblings, born less than one year apart. Aki Jamal Durham met the Pullen brothers while he and Wesley were freshmen at Peabody High School in Pittsburgh, Pennsylvania. Greg El came to know the brothers upon entering as a freshman into The Linsly School in West Virginia, where Dwight was a sophomore. They were later joined by Wesley at Linsly, who transferred there in his sophomore year. The four drew closer while in college. During that time, each of them participated in the INROADS college internship program, which brought the young men together at weekend trainings every summer.

The DAWG team formed as a Master Mind group in 2006, at Greg's suggestion, and the exchange of positive energy, critical and caring feedback, and accountability has been invaluable to each individual member. It was this new way of sharing with one another that lead to the creation of the Spider Web Philosophy and the collaboration of coauthoring this book.

They are available for speaking engagements, corporate trainings, and consulting opportunities, demonstrating the power of purposeful relationships and how they create self-sustaining growth in any environment, culture, or industry.

https://www.facebook.com/SWPdreamcatcher
@SWPdreamcatcher

Dwight Pullen

Dwight H. Pullen, Jr. is a Transportation Executive, focused on Airport Infrastructure with a global full-service engineering company.

As a Global Market Leader for Aviation, Dwight led strategy, profitability and market penetration. As a Program Manager, he led the following Capital Programs: Denver International Airport's South Terminal Redevelopment Program ($500 million), the Abu Dhabi International Airport Expansion Program ($7.6 Billion) in the United Arab Emirates and the 5th Runway expansion ($1.2 billion) at the Hartsfield-Jackson Atlanta International Airport.

Dwight received his B.S. in Civil Engineering from the University of Pittsburgh; he is an alum of the Georgia Institute of Technology. He has a passion for Science Technology, Engineering and Math (STEM) and ensuring that inner city communities are exposed to the STEM fields.

Dwight's has served on many non-profit boards and civic organizations in the Atlanta metro area and in the Denver metro area.

Dwight is passionate about Marketplace Leadership. He models his approach to leadership in business (the Marketplace) after his mentor, John Maxwell. Impacting lives, motivating teams and transforming organizations is his chief objective. Leadership is a process marked by constant growth. Dwight strives to empower people to live out leadership.

A native of Pittsburgh, PA, Dwight is the husband of Eleanore and the father of four sons, Dwight III, Blake, Grant and Devon. Dwight and his family live in Denver, CO.

@dhpullen
ch2m.com

Aki Jamal Durham

Aki Jamal Durham is a self-described "serial entrepreneur and right brained individual with left brained training and sensibilities." He maintains his interest and work in the arts recording voice-overs, acting, working as a graphic design, and serving a professional master of ceremonies.

Passionate about people and their well-being, Aki has a gift for understanding and discerning relationships that he longs to share. He is the founder of Intentional Relationship Services, which offers relationship coaching and consulting services that fuel and accelerate growth through greater self-awareness and purposeful relationship building for individuals, couples, groups, organizations, and businesses. Aki has more than fifteen years of experience in the managing, brokering, and coaching of relationships for corporations in the experiential marketing, beverage, and finance industries. He works with TWOgether Pittsburgh as an outreach coordinator and program manager creating and maintaining social-media content, forming and managing partnerships with local nonprofits and churches, and facilitating marriage and relationship education programming.

His time and skills are given to the community through board participation and design committee involvement for Mt. Ararat Baptist Church, INROADS/Pittsburgh, Pittsburgh Urban Christian School, and the POISE Foundation.

Aki attended the University of Pittsburgh from 1989 to 1992 and studied business management before transferring to Hampton University, where he earned a BS in business management in 1995. He is presently working toward a master's degree in human services with an emphasis in marriage and family therapy at Liberty University. A proud father and loving husband, Aki lives in Pittsburgh with his wife, Aliya, and their son and daughter, Deacon and Coley.

@AkiJamal
nowcasting.com/akijamal
intentionalrelationships.info

Wesley Pullen

Wesley G. Pullen is the General Manager & Vice President of the Deployment Solutions business within Electric Cloud. This business unit is responsible for the Application Release Automation (ARA)/

Deployment Automation portfolio of solutions. He has over 20 years of experience in software development methodologies and design standards and has applied this experience to the commercial and private sector. His ability to take complex tasks and objectives and simplify them into actionable goals is unique. He has traveled to China, Singapore, Turkey, Austria, Israel, Germany, Ireland, London, Spain, Romania, Australia, and over 45 states within the continental USA teaching, mentoring, and advising leaders in management and executive management on business concepts and strategies around Business Automation, Application Release Automation (ARA), DevOps, Big Data and Cloud solutions.

Prior to working for Electric Cloud, Wesley was the Vice President of the Emerging Solutions Group & Global ARA Solutions Group within Automic Software (formerly UC4 Software). Here he was able to build a world-class Deployment Automation solution and business practice along with managing the cloud portfolio strategy and solution as well. Wesley has also held leadership roles at BMC Software (as Director of Solutions Architecture), Department of Defense (Executive Advisor & Chief Technical Testing Expert), Biz Lending Solutions (Executive Board Member), and IBM (Technical Engagement Mgr).

Wesley's passion is around leadership (student of the John Maxwell Leadership Series) and innovation (student of the Geoffrey A. Moore Escape Velocity Framework). He has worked with several venture capital firms, private equity firms, and technology boards to help them expand their technology footprint, become more innovative, and accomplish financial goals through strategic acquisitions.

Wesley also mentors young men through programs like AMI (A Moment of Impact), Investing NOW, and Legacy in Pennsylvania. Wesley received his B.S. in Electrical Engineering from the University of Pittsburgh.

Wesley has served and continues to serve on non-profit boards and technology start-ups in the Metro-DC area. Also a native of Pittsburgh, PA,

Wesley is the father of four wonderful kids, Emmanuel, Evan, Elyse, and Eaden and lives in the Baltimore Metro area.

@WesleyGPullen
electric-cloud.com

Greg El

Greg El has over 20 years of experience as an entrepreneur, business consultant, and community advocate.

Greg is a loving husband, devoted father and co-founder of TriZen LLC – a Philadelphia based DBE Certified Business Consulting and Leadership Development Company. TriZen designs and facilitates training, coaching, and leadership development programs that help organizations and individuals develop and refine their leadership capabilities and potential.

Greg's areas of focus are Leadership Development and Strategic Management. His unique combination of management consulting and human capital development experience helps organizations and individuals create and implement strategies that improve performance.

Prior to TriZen Greg was a member of PricewaterhouseCoopers where he worked in the Audit and Business Advisory Services Group. After PWC he joined CIGNA Corporation where he graduated from the highly regarded Financial Management Development Program. Through these two world-class organizations, Greg amassed a number of valuable experiences and responsibilities such as: executing business and strategic plans, benchmarking and prioritizing capital expenditures, analyzing competitive pricing, participating in the due diligence efforts of mergers and acquisitions, and implementing financial process improvements in Hong Kong, Taiwan, South Korea, Brazil, and Chile.

Greg is also the CEO of a real estate investment firm – Circle Seven LLC. He sits on the board the People's Emergency Center and is a Big Brother with Big Brothers Big Sisters Southeastern Pennsylvania. Greg is a certified public accountant and received his B.S. in Business Administration and Accounting from Temple University. He lives in Philadelphia with his wife, Lauren and their son Gregory 'Eli'.

@wmgregel
@TriZenLLC
trizeninc.com

Works Cited

Books

Hill, Napoleon. *The Law of Success in Sixteen Lessons*. Cleveland, Ohio: Ralston University Press, 1928.

Hill, Napoleon. *Think and Grow Rich*. Cleveland, Ohioa: The Ralston Society, 1937.

Julian, Larry. *God Is My CEO—Following God's Principles in a Bottom-Line World*.Avon, Massachuesettes: Adams Media, 2001.

Lechter, Sharon L., and Greg S. Reid. *Think and Grow Rich: Three Feet from Gold—Turn Your Obstacles into Opportunities*. New York, New York: Sterling, 2009.

Maxwell, John C. *Leadership GOLD*. Nashville, Tennessee: Thomas Nelson, 2008.

Articles

Dye, Lee. "Spider Web Holds Valuable Secrets." Written for ABCNews.com (September 4, 2011). http://abcnews.go.com/Technology/story?id=97539&page=1#.T1pmkoEgfTo.

Maxwell, John C. "In Finding Your Purpose: Identifying Your Strengths and Going for Growth." *SUCCESS* (August 2009). http://www.successmagazine.com/finding-your-purpose/PARAMS/article/290/channel/1519.

Online

Darling, Daniel. "Five Ways to Find a Mentor." Michael Hyatt—Intentional Leadership. January 27, 2012. http://michaelhyatt.com/five-ways-to-find-a-mentor.html.

Darling, Daniel. January 27, 2012. http://www.danieldarling.com.

Hayashi, Cheryl. "The Magnificence of Spider Silk." Speech. YouTube. TED Talks. December 7, 2011. http://www.youtube.com/watch?v=xossR6eHv3I. January 27, 2012. http://www.stjude.tv/danny_thomas_story.cfm.

Made in the USA
Middletown, DE
08 February 2019